sweeping buffing dusting polishing waxing
vacuuming baking beating blending chopping grating slicing dicing mixing
making cleaning cooking freezing
squeezing peeling blanching boi-
ling broiling roasting broasting
simmering steaming sauteeing
poaching frying browning burning oiling creaming folding
whipping pureeing icing frosting adding cooling measuring
scooping scrubbing stacking sorting
starching scalding bleaching
folding ironing straightening
washing hemming mending
crocheting knitting quilting knot-
ting macrame embroidering
sewing needlepointing stitching
soaking drying hanging all done

also by **Karen Finley**

Shock Treatment

Enough Is Enough

LIVING IT UP

Karen Finley

DOUBLEDAY

New York   London   Toronto

Sydney   Auckland

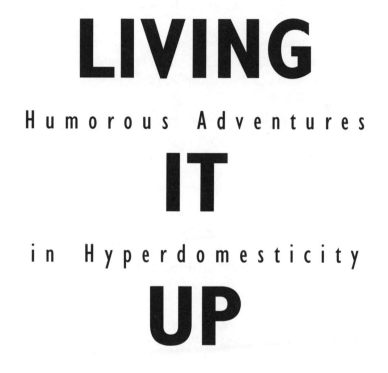

LIVING

Humorous Adventures

IT

in Hyperdomesticity

UP

⚓

PUBLISHED BY DOUBLEDAY
a division of
Bantam Doubleday Dell Publishing Group, Inc.
1540 Broadway, New York, New York 10036

DOUBLEDAY and the portrayal of an anchor
with a dolphin are trademarks of Doubleday
a division of Bantam Doubleday Dell Publishing Group, Inc.

Library of Congress Cataloging-in-Publication Data
Finley, Karen.
Living it up : humorous adventures in hyperdomesticity /
Karen Finley. — 1st ed.
p.   cm.
1. Stewart, Martha—Parodies, imitations, etc.   2. United States—
Social life and customs—1971-   —Humor.   3. American wit and humor.
I. Martha Stewart living.   II. Title.
PN6231.P3F56   1996
818'.5407—dc20   96-14973
CIP

For my mother
Mary
with love

Dear Friends,

I know and fully understand how guilty we feel that we aren't making something out of nothing constantly in our hectic lives. For instance, you know how hard it must have been for Marcia Clark to have made dinner while in court every day. Well, while everyone was looking at her skirt length, I was looking at the court table, and I thought, "There has got to be room for a Crock-Pot!"

Here is my recipe for

Court Crock-Pot Stew.

Go to Automat in court and buy everything for $10.00 in quarters (1 roll). Peanut butter on cheese crackers, tortilla chips, microwave Beefaroni, popcorn, and pretzels. Place in Crock-Pot filled with water from the drinking fountain and 4 chicken bouillon cubes.

Most people carry emergency provisions in their car—well, I don't go anywhere without my trusty Teflon convertible Crock-Pot. "What does it convert to?" you ask. Well, you can do several small loads of wash, last night's dishes, and most importantly, CROCK-POT STEW! All while making opening remarks, closing statements, examinations, etc., etc. . . .

I also have AT ALL TIMES a 100-foot bright orange UTILITY extension cord for those hard to reach/hard to get to/down the hall/behind the jury, judge, or opposing lawyers OUTLETS. If you thought moving the sofa every time you VACUUM is hard—just imagine moving an entire jury and alternates. I carry a good long extension cord to plug in the Crock-Pot.

After lunch: Take half-eaten sandwiches, celery, carrots from leftover lunches—french fries—stick in stew.

If anyone objects to the Crock-Pot say, "You don't want me to make dinner for my kids?" That'll shut 'em up.

Drive home in car with Crock-Pot in lap, on pillow or purse—keep it away from those court papers.

Ladle stew in bowls with lots of Parmesan cheese. KIDS WILL LOVE IT!

Here in *Living It Up* I invite you to join me in humorous adventures in hyperdomesticity.

Karen Finley

January

Resolutions

I like to start the year off with a New Year's Day Resolution Party. I invite one person to the house and I psychologically rip her to shreds to point out what needs to be resolved in her life. She is never going to resolve her own problems, so I do the resolving for her. I tell her, "I'm sick and tired of hearing you bitch about your job, your family, your relationship." Then I take over her life and make telephone calls for her. I tell her father-in-law to go to hell. I announce a divorce to a spouse. I quit her job for her. Yes, it's tense. But it is so much fun.

SMILE, You JUST TOLD YOUR BEST Friend's FATHER IN LAW TO GO TO HELL!

Sometimes when the personal life is awful, the living quarters are as well, so it means I go to her house and rearrange the furniture, tear down the curtains, throw out that dog-pee-stained rug. She is devastated, but she'll never be the same once I get through her closet. The look on her face when I throw out some shirt she still boasts about wearing since high school. OUT!

eyes big when quitting a job for a friend

I extend this resolution service to all my friends. I send New Year's Resolution cards to friends, family, and acquaintances. I make them from recycled Christmas cards and wrapping paper. I write personal resolutions for each person on the inside of the card. I send out cards that say "This year try not to chill the red wine" or "This year bring a hostess gift when I invite you to dinner" or "Once you take a bite out of a cracker or piece of celery, please don't return it to the onion dip even if it's only family." "This year get call waiting" is one of my favorites. I sign the cards—Resolution Now.

My Very Own
New Year's Brunch

I like to start the menu out with this hangover helper.

First you need to get your hands on some blood. That is going to be tricky. Try butcher shops, hospitals, and morticians, or drive around, looking for roadkill. Boil blood. Cool. Mix blood with equal parts of Hungarian Bulls' Blood Wine. Crush and dissolve a beef bouillon cube with a little hot water per serving. Fill glasses with ice. Pour 2 shots of peppered vodka over ice and bouillon. Fill with blood mixture. Add 2 dashes of Tabasco sauce. Garnish with celery and sprinkle with salt and pepper. Now, that's what I call a killer Bloody Mary.

Make a dip out of mayonnaise, eggnog, and crushed peppermints to accompany their sipping.

While your guests are waking up, get this in the oven.

Happy New Year's
Breakfast Casserole

Butter casserole dish generously. It's New Year's, for God's sake! Cover bottom of casserole with 2 inches of Frosted Flakes. Pour 8 beaten eggs with 8 tbs. of Tang over flakes. Using spoon carefully, spoon pancake batter onto flakes. Sprinkle with bacon bits. Bake for 45 minutes in 350-degree oven.

Or make omelets with chocolate and peanut butter.
Serve with a salad of marinated pine needles and croutons of stale fruitcake.

Decorations

Get the hot-glue gun out, people! Cover walls with red velvet and ermine for that Dr. Zhivago look. Give a disgusted look to whoever is not old enough to remember the movie.

Pine Needles

So the holidays are over and you don't know what to do with those thousands of dried, prickly pine needles that are all over your house after Christmas? You find them under the radiator, under the chair, in the carpet. I've spent many hours from January until April pondering those beasties. I once spent an entire New Year's Eve thinking about what to do with those green devils, and the answer was—Underwear Sachets!

pine needle underwear sachet is unisex

Sure they're un-comfortable, but they sure smell good. I like wearing them right when I get out of the shower. It gives you that extra freshness that you need.

Making them is easy. Take 2 pairs of underwear (try to make sure that they are the same size and *never* try to match a bikini with a brief), put one pair in-

don't try this with a bikini! OUCH!

side of the other and sew or staple the legs together, then stuff with the pine needles that you have swept up and then sew or staple together the waistbands.

I love to wear them and they're a good insurance policy if you've just eaten a plate full of beans and have too much gas. They act like an OdorEater for your pants.

Of course there are other projects to fill your time involving pine needles. I always get complaints from friends and neighbors telling me that they can't ever get all the pine needles up from the carpet. They say, "Karen, I've tried Christmas tree bags, power diesel vacuums, and hand-picking each needle. I've made 2 pairs of Underwear Sachets for every person in my Rolodex, but it's July and I'm still picking up those damn needles!" Well, of course I've never had this problem, because I say—just leave the damn needles there! In fact, what I do is actually take in old pine trees from the curb, where others have thrown them out, and I shake all their old needles all over my house.

Accentuate! I put pine needles on the floor and in the corners. Sometimes I try to create hills and valleys of needles ranging from several inches to several feet. I have gotten very good at making pine-needle landscapes behind my furniture or right in the middle of the living room rug. Have fun. Be creative. Soon you'll be hearing "I feel like I'm in the woods" from friends who visit your loft in the city even though you live in an industrial park. Then you'll know that you've made a very, very country home.

January Extra

Food—Vodka snow Slurpees

Clothes—Glue cotton balls to your clothes for that extra-wintry snow-scene look.

Party—Don't know what to do this weekend? Too cold outside? Turn the entire house into an ice skating rink! Here's how: The night before the party, turn off the heat in your house or apartment and flood the entire first floor or basement by turning on the hose or letting a sink or bathtub overflow. Keep that heat off and make sure it's below freezing by opening up window and doors. It takes a while, but it will freeze. Then get all bundled up. Bring out the extra blankets. It's going to be a cold night. Go to sleep. Yes, it's cold when you wake up, but just think, you've got an ice skating rink!

Invite people over. The neighbors won't believe it.
Make vodka snow Slurpees from the ice you sledgehammer out.

glue
cotton
balls
to
clothes
for a
WINTER
LOOK

Redecorating the Bathroom

Having my skating party put me in the mood to put these two ladies to work. This year I'm totally redecorating my downstairs bathroom with the infamous skaters Nancy Kerrigan and Tanya Harding as the theme. I have totally redecorated my downstairs guest bathroom with Nancy Kerrigan and Tanya Harding as the theme. I must admit that I was looking for an excuse to use these two charming ladies, and what an inspiration they have turned out to be!

First, I've hung skates from the ceiling. I've focused little mini-halogen spotlights on the skates. Do they make wonderful shadows on the wall. It also makes a beautiful nitelite for my guests to find their way into the bathroom at night.

Next, I've hand-painted onto the toilet lid the scene of Nancy's knee being clubbed at the skating rink. Under the lid I've painted Tonya pleading with the judges about her broken lace. And on the seat itself I've painted the two skating around the seat. It's absolutely fabulous! A toilet was meant for these two.

I've carried that theme over to the walls, where I've made a stencil of skating skirts and baseball bats that I ring around the walls just above the wainscoting. And I've color-Xeroxed their skating outfits that I've cut out of magazines and had them transferred to tiles for the shower.

In redecorating, it's always the details that count, so for hand towels I've hand-embroidered one with the image of Tanya and one with the image of Nancy. And for that finishing touch, on the side of the toilet I leave Magic Markers so guests can illustrate and graffiti comments about the duo. I find it is a more original approach than a stuffy old guest book.

The Tonya & Nancy Toilet Seat

TONYA COMPLAINING TO JUDGES HER SKATES LACES ARE BROKEN

JUDGES

SKATING TONYA

SKATING NANCY

NANCY AND CLUBBED LEGS

WHITE LIKE ICERINK

there is nothing quite like lying under the bed with our prized possessions

February is a dark, bleak, cold month with short, depressing days. Nothing happens in February. I admit, yes, even I get depressed. I try to fill my life with constant things to do and plan, but it still creeps up on me. So what I've done is create a depression room. We have places in our house to read, to sleep, to eat, to take in the mail, but for a truly contemporary life it is necessary to facilitate our moods. It is time to serve the needs of depression. Decorating should reflect and facilitate our lows as well as our highs. I think it's best just to wallow in your depression, and I feel that it's a good idea to give that wallowing its own space. If you don't have enough room where you live, use a closet or go under the bed. Wallpaper the walls or underneath the bed with photos of depressed people like Sylvia Plath or any depressed relatives. Sometimes for a change I wallpaper the depression room with pictures of overcast, cloudy, bleak, dreary, gray skies.

For relief I go under my bed and hide and hold my KitchenAid mixer and my daily calendar till I feel better. Just being around my mixer makes me feel better. Forget friends, give me an object that accomplishes something well.

Or I go sit in one of my closets and feel my closet organizational system with my Dewey decimal hanger filing system for my sweaters, skirts, shirts, slacks, and scarves. I feel better because I remember my accomplishment.

I KNOW WHERE EVERYTHING IS IN MY CLOSET.

Then I go into my depression room, which I designed especially for times like these.

I paint the room totally black with a matte paint. NO SHINY BLACK PAINT PLEASE! Then I make a personal altar to everything that makes me feel good, that gives me a sense of purpose. I include my coffee grinder, my cappuccino maker, my stain removers, my double-stick tape, my super-thin, long vacuum attachment to reach in those hard-to-get places like radiators, my

KitchenAid blender, my waxed-wood lemon juicer, my rain hat that says DO IT that I bought at a garage sale in Sag Harbor, and my years and years of lists, and I meditate on the art of doing and feel alive again.

The black walls become a chalkboard. With colored chalk I write lists of things that need to be done.

the depression room

I look forward to Q-TIPPING the dirt in the crack of stairs!

Q-Tipping the dirt from the corners of the stairs

paint broom handle to go with kitchen

decoupage under hood of car

ideas for my new book on Egyptian cooking, *What to Cook in a Tomb—Buried Before Your Time*

100 things to do with pesto and dried tomatoes

I love to make lists. I make lists and lists of all sorts of things to do—for the month, for the year. I make lists for all my friends, for the government, for movie stars. And soon I'm no longer depressed! I have so many things to do! You won't believe what making a list does for my outlook. Then I frame my favorite lists. They make an excellent conversation piece and ensure that your friends and neighbors will know that you are constantly busy doing something.

Do Your Own Casket

It has been during this bleak, dark month that got me thinking about the ultimate hibernation. I've come to realize that I just can't trust anyone to correctly organize my funeral after I'm gone. Many people fear death, but my biggest fear is that my last appearance will be lying in an ordinary, nondescript, unmemorable casket. I want people walking away from my funeral with tears in their eyes, saying, "That was the most beautiful, amazingly decorated casket I've ever seen."

The only way to ensure a funeral to my liking is to plan and rehearse my own funeral. People rehearse for weddings, take birthing classes, where they practice breathing, practice baking a cake till they get it just right. So every year I rehearse my funeral with me center stage. I send out invitations, and it has become an annual event with guests even sending funeral wreaths and flowers. I always update the ceremony to keep up with the latest funereal trends, although I'm having a great influence, I have to say, on funereal decoration. Let's get funerals and caskets a little more wild, please! A funeral director is going to tell me what the best-looking casket is? No way.

I design and do all the flowers for the rehearsal and invite my friends and family. It's a little hard on Mother, but I like the tears for effect. I also cook all the food and decide on the music—I want everything to be just right! And right means *my* way.

In my home I have a freezer just for food I make for my funeral party. You never can tell when the day will arrive, so it is good to be prepared. I always have a cake for 250 people just waiting in the wings of my freezer for that unexpected wedding or funeral. Then on the wedding cake, I decorate with fresh roses. I ice my funeral cake in a midnight-blue or dark purple and cover with dried roses. I love to go gothic for funerals! Select a theme for your big day. Try a come-as-you-are funeral, where guests come dressed as they are when they hear the news of your passing. Or do a medieval pageant or go Egyptian. Have your body wrapped as a mummy with your favorite aprons, clothes, and gardening gloves. I cook and design a menu with written instructions on the freezer bags. On the inside of the freezer lid I draw how I want the tables to look and write down what dishes to use with a marker.

I even make my own casket, and I'll share the plans with you right now. To make your own personal casket, lie on a piece of 4 × 8 plywood (make sure that it's a thick piece so that your dead weight doesn't make you fall through when they pick you up in it) and have a friend draw an outline of your body. Cut out a casket-type shape around the body outline, nail on some side pieces, and hinge another casket shape for the top, and you have a great base on which to decorate your own personalized casket. Now, why does a casket have to be a rectangle? Get creative. It's now or never. Try an outline of a body shape, a butterfly, an oval, a scalloped edge.

I've lined the inside of my casket with handmade velvet from France that I've bleached, dyed, and detailed with lace made by nuns in Belgium. I stained the exterior with a turquoise stain that I made up myself from my blue delphiniums. Next I spray-paint dried pasta and macaroni gold. I choose bows, wagon wheels, and elbows. Using my hot-glue gun reserved only for this occasion, I glue the macaroni in an abstract pattern. But you can arrange the macaroni to form words or sayings. And for that extra special, personal touch I dried some of the hydrangea from my garden and made an arrangement that will cover the top. It's more exquisite than any store-bought casket. I know the guests at my open-casket wake will appreciate the time and hard work that has gone into creating my final resting spot.

Next year I think I'm going to make my casket out of some old weathered-looking barn siding. I love the look of distressed wood,

MAKING YOUR VERY OWN CASKET

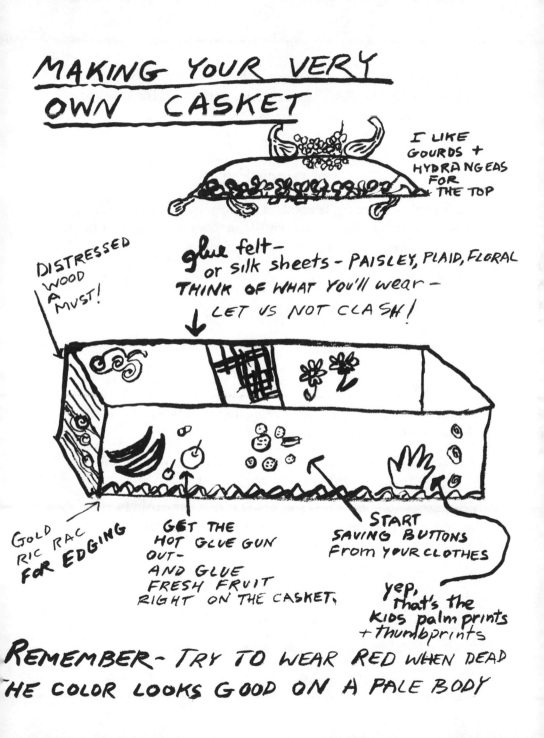

I LIKE GOURDS + HYDRANGEAS FOR THE TOP

DISTRESSED WOOD A MUST!

glue felt — or silk sheets — PAISLEY, PLAID, FLORAL
THINK OF WHAT YOU'LL wear —
LET US NOT CLASH!

GOLD RIC RAC for EDGING

GET THE HOT GLUE GUN OUT — AND GLUE FRESH FRUIT RIGHT ON THE CASKET.

START SAVING BUTTONS FROM YOUR CLOTHES

yep, that's the KIDS palm prints + thumbprints

REMEMBER — TRY TO WEAR RED WHEN DEAD
HE COLOR LOOKS GOOD ON A PALE BODY

and I can't wait to hear everyone ask, "Where did you find that beautiful antique casket?" And I'll answer from my lying-down position, "I made it myself."

February Extra

Remember—There are fewer days in this month, so keep your depression to a working minimum. Remember to work two hours more each day to get an entire REAL month in.

Valentine's Day

February 14 Daily Calendar

5:30 A.M.—I don't want to get up. No one cares about my thirty-foot coconut cake heart with cherry butter cream inside.

6:00 A.M.—Turn on *The Today Show.* I should be on that show making hydrangea hearts.

Turn on *Good Morning America.* I should be on that show making portobello mushrooms glazed in white chocolate.

6:30 A.M.—Roll under bed and hold on to KitchenAid blender and stay there for rest of the day till feeling better. Admit it. I'm depressed. I hate Valentine's Day.

Noon—Start thinking about creative projects that can be done with slush.

1:00 P.M.—Well, you can't eat slush—too dirty.

2:00 P.M.—Well, you can't wear slush—too cold.

3:00 P.M.—Well, you can't decorate with slush—too slippery.

4:00 P.M.—Well, you can't entertain with slush—too unpredictable.

5:00 P.M.—Oh, my God, it's Valentine's Day and I'm lying under this bed!

5:05 P.M.—Hand-deliver chocolate hearts to every neighbor for a one-and-a-half-mile radius. Just happen to have a freezer full of bittersweet chocolate hearts I made when I had some free time.

6:00 P.M.—Take out frozen pizzas. Cut into hearts. Broil. Cover with strawberry ice cream.

7:00 P.M.—Serve to pets. I'm not too hungry. Nibble on a Slim Jim.

7:13 P.M.—Start calling ex-lovers, and when they answer hang up.

8:00 P.M.—Wear giant hydrangea heart costume in car, playing love songs on full volume on the stereo.

8:30 P.M.—Stop in to supermarket wearing heart costume to pick up Oreos, Ring Dings, and a quart of beer.

9:00 P.M.—I guess it's time to use my valentine-heart-shaped Jacuzzi with my scented candles that I made myself out of old crayons in the shapes of cupids, hearts, and flowers. The wallpaper is silk-screened with the script from *Love Story.*

9:30 P.M.—Crew over to document, film, and photograph for my next book—*Art of the Heart*—*Redoing Your Bathroom in the Name of Love.*

Later—Good night!

March

When I give a divorce party, I prefer the month of March. It's the rain, the mud, the cloudy days, the nimble crocus being destroyed by the weight of the snow that gives a March divorce some distinction. Like June is for weddings, March should be for divorce.

I have found March to be a terrific time to give a party. After a hard winter of the battling couple cooped up together, I know that they're ready for a messy little divorce party. Everyone involved gets in a pissy mood, sides are taken, lawyers and families arguing—who's going to get the stereo? Who's going to get the arts and crafts pottery? You know. You've been there.

I feel that what is missing from divorce is a good ritual. It is essential that the divorcing couple take vows, and that is just one of the functions the divorce party provides. I don't mean renew their wedding vows; I'm talking about taking new divorce vows. Examples of some of the more common vows are:

"I promise to call you twelve times a day."

"I promise to go out with my ex-wife's girlfriend."

"I promise to go out with my ex-husband's boss."

I also believe in having maids of dishonor, worst man, etc., present at the divorce party. Be creative. The ritual of giving back the gifts is one of my favorites. Here, the ex-couple give back all the stupid gifts they received (except for money, because the lawyers will get all of that). They can auction them off or guests can have a grab bag.

As for the setting, I always like to have the divorce party right

where the unhappy couple lived. It's more personal. For food at the party I say just order pizza. Since there is so much tension going on in the room, you want to get everyone in and out as quickly as possible. This way you don't need table settings, and as soon as the fighting breaks out, everyone can still grab a slice and get the hell out of there. For flowers I think a cactus is appropriate.

Entertainment is essential. I call the entertainment *This Marriage Is Over.* Usually two guests dress up as the couple and perform short skits through out the house (bathroom, bedroom, car, or on the phone) based on their failed marriage. Other guests can get involved playing themselves—neighbors, relatives, coworkers, or shopkeepers for those steamy scenes in public. I create versions of *This Marriage Is Over.* Guests can compete as the arguing couple. The divorcing couple are the judges. Or try charades, again based on the ended marriage. The subjects are endless—Intimate Moments, The Fight, Property, Jealousy, Money.

If you want to get the tears flowing, set up a museum or relic room. Here, display the wedding dress and photographs. Recreate the wedding cake. If there is film or video, have it projected lifesize. If not, blow up a photo. Have a guest book in the room for people to make comments: "I don't think we will see you after today" "Good luck" "I'm on my fifth marriage, so I don't know what to say" "Join the club!"

March Extras

Here are some of the St. Patrick's Day traditions we do in my family. I've created a drink that keeps to the spirit of St. Patrick but still keeps up with the daily vitamins. It's important to keep your strength up. Parties can be strenuous!

Shamrock HOUSE COZY

Leprechaun Cocktail

I prefer the texture of frozen vegetables to fresh.
1 lb. frozen broccoli
1 lb. frozen chopped spinach
10 oz. frozen peas
1 lb. frozen French-cut beans
1 liter crème de menthe

Put all ingredients in blender. Blend well. Pour over ice in frosted mugs. Garnish with mint.

Have a little extra time? Knit an entire shamrock to cover your house like a tea cozy.

In Chicago there is a tradition of turning the Chicago River green. Try turning your water green. Just tape bottles of food coloring underneath the faucets. Make a slow drip.

Will your guests think they had too much Leprechaun Cocktail when they wash their hands!

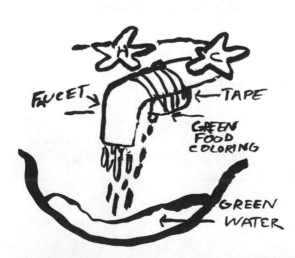

Shamrock house cozy

St. Patrick's Day

March 17 Daily Calendar

5:00 A.M.—Start the day with a Leprechaun Cocktail and a lime-green Jell-O moisturizing bath.

6:00 A.M.—Get out of Jell-O before it sets.

6:15 A.M.—Change into 18th-century milkmaid costume for my

new video *HOW TO MILK YOUR HYBRID GOATS AND COWS AND STILL LOOK GOOD.*

8:00 A.M.—While crew is cleaning up, spray hydrangeas green.

8:30 A.M.—Make green eggs and ham for crew.

9:00 A.M.—I don't understand why people won't eat green eggs and ham. Well, maybe it was the green mint toast with green raisins that put them off.

9:30 A.M.—Slap apple cider vinegar on skin, for skin is irritated from Jell-O bath.

9:45 A.M.—Hand-sculpt and whittle leprechauns and shamrocks out of Irish Spring soap.

10:30 A.M.—Remember to talk all day with Irish brogue till it gets on people's nerves.

10:45 A.M.—Remember answer phone with "Top o' the Morning."

10:50 A.M.—Make sure answering machine is playing "Danny Boy" on the personal phone and "When Irish Eyes Are Smiling" on the business phone. Have subliminal message underneath, saying, buy this woman an emerald.

11:10 A.M.—I am really behind schedule. Have another Leprechaun Cocktail and hang leprechaun and shamrock soap sculptures from ceiling or make mobile.

Noon—Get those Irish soda breads going now!

12:30 P.M.—Think about if there is anything you can do with slush for 10 minutes.

12:40 P.M.—I'm going to need help from the wee people. I'm having a divorce party for my niece who got married here in January.

12:45 P.M.—Well, my niece and her ex-husband are getting a St. Patrick's Day party.

12:50 P.M.—Start corned beef, cabbage, and boiled potatoes and carrots for one hundred.

1:30 P.M.—Spray-paint entire house green. Takes twenty cans. Always buy in bulk!

2:00 P.M.—Take St. Patrick's float out of garage for town parade.

2:30 P.M.—Children and parents arrive. Costumes already laid out for them to wear. Children wear leprechaun outfits. Parents wear rainbow costumes. Pets wear pot-of-gold costumes. I wear green hydrangea shamrock costume that is two stories tall.

3:00 P.M.—Drive car float of giant shamrock teapot that pours tea in origami cups made from imported Irish grass made into handmade paper.

3:30 P.M.—In parade.

4:30 P.M.—Run home.

4:45 P.M.—Guests for divorce party already arrived and have helped themselves to Leprechaun Cocktail.

5:30 P.M.—Serve corned beef and cabbage and Irish soda bread. It's a little burnt. Tell them it's caramelized. Use paper plates.

5:45 P.M.—Frost green cupcakes with arugula butter cream frosting

5:50 P.M.—My niece starts yelling at me that this is supposed to be her divorce party, not a St. Patrick's Day party. What does she want from me? I have my reputation to uphold. You think I'm supposed to ignore a holiday like St. Patrick's Day because she is getting divorced? Do you think there is any other holiday this month? What the hell can you come up with for the Ides of March? Or, worse, Women's History Month. Who cares? What the hell can you make with hydrangeas for the Ides of March or, worse, for Women's History Month?

6:00 P.M.—The shamrock float returns from the parade.

6:05 P.M.—40 kids, 30 parents, 12 dogs, and 2 cats NOW EXPECT TO EAT!

6:06 P.M.—All the corned beef and cabbage is gone. What, the divorce party ate seconds? How dare they!

6:07 P.M.—Time to make green eggs and ham and green mint toast with green raisins.

6:30 P.M.—I don't believe it, but they are eating it except the cats. If you are hungry enough . . .

7:00 P.M.—Time to turn on the green knitted tea cozy that covers the entire outside of the house and lights up.

7:15 P.M.—Serve cupcakes and Leprechaun Cocktails.

7:30 P.M.—Put on green hydrangea shamrock costume and join my niece and her ex-husband dancing Irish jig.

8:00 P.M.—Give demonstration in home via satellite and Internet of knitting an Irish fisherman's sweater that covers the entire city of Belfast with enough wool left over for small dogs over the age of 11 to have their own sweater too.

9:05 P.M.—Divorce party—niece is cutting up her wedding dress and I suggest she weave a nice bedspread out of it.

10:00 P.M.—Everyone home. Go upstairs and have another Jell-O bath.

April Fool's Day is an underused and underexpressed holiday. In my neighborhood I plan to do something about it. I start off the day with mooning. I ring my neighbors' doorbells and then flash them my derriere that has some catchy phrase written on it like Butt of Jokes or Moon River.

I like to make my April Fool pranks special, even for the teenagers. Instead of letting them out of the house with any old toilet paper to make streamers in the neighbors' trees down the street, I hand-paint and tie-dye the rolls to give it a special Woodstock, hippie, Grateful Dead look. I also stencil-paint their eggs before they go out egging. This causes a jealous rage in some parents. Well, at least I think it's a jealous rage.

hand paint toilet paper for making tree streamers

April Fools!

I love prank phone calls. Here are some ideas for prank calls to be made to your favorite gourmet store:

"Is your Brie running? . . . You better go catch it!"

"This is Popeye. I hear you've been using olive oil."

"How sour is your sourdough bread?" . . . "Well, you better go sweeten it up."

"May I speak with Basil Notsofresh?"

Since we are talking about pranks, I think I will share with you a little bit of foolery. April means spring flowers, so it's time to start the damn gardening again. Who has time for gardening in April? So I learned this little trick from my friend Muney Rivers. Every year I take out my plastic daffodils and tulips from the attic, wash

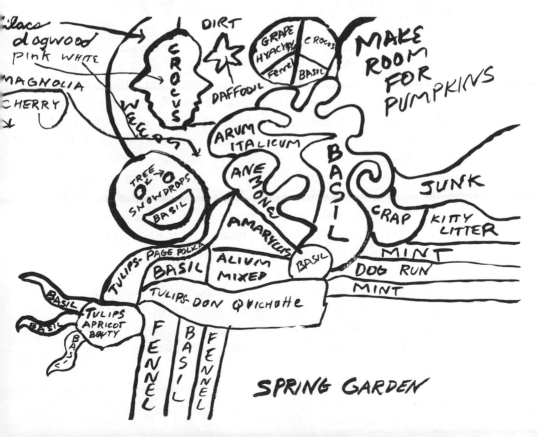

Remember the GARDEN IS
LIKE A RORSCHACH TEST
DON'T EVER GIVE
ANYTHING AWAY!

off the dust and dirt, and stick them in the ground in the middle of the night. Everyone thinks that I'm such a great gardener, but my secret is that I don't let them near my spring gardens. From a distance, fake grape hyacinths look magnificent, but I am getting worried because my Rembrandt red plastic tulips are fading and now that the local Woolworth's is closed, I am having a hard time replacing them.

For some gardens on my property I don't even bother with the formality of planting plastic flowers. I just draw on a chalkboard a huge garden map of how I would like my garden to be planted for June (if I had any desire to do that sort of thing). Then I just write in big letters "USE YOUR IMAGINATION." I have to credit that purple dinosaur, Barney, for that one.

I map out where azaleas, magnolias, dogwoods, lilacs, lilies of the valley, and roses, etc., should be. People always feel as if they're getting a peek at some future spot of beauty on my property, but unless I find a new plastic flower supplier, the same sign will be out there next year.

with not too much TROUBLE YOUR ROACHES CAN LOOK LIKE BUNNIES!

April Extra

Looking for a good idea for a centerpiece for that special spring or Easter dinner? I got this idea from my friend, the late artist David Wognarowicz. Collect roaches. Cut small bunny ears out of white and pink construction paper. Then glue bunny ears and cotton tails on the appropriate anatomical area of the roaches. Let scamper on table or place in clear plastic shoe box. Now, that's what I call a centerpiece!

NOW THIS IS WHAT I CALL A CENTERPIECE!

My Very Own
April Fool's Press Conference

I have called upon you today, all editors and writers for women's magazines, and to members of the press who have been interested in my pursuit of domesticity, to make a very important announcement.

I have been doing a lot of soul searching and I have come to the conclusion that my entire career has been a sham. I've come to realize that my lifetime work devoted to taking control of the creative power in the home has set back women one hundred years. I have exploited the fact that the only acceptable power a woman can have without ostracism is in the home, and I profited from this sexism. I knowingly knew that since women can't be truly recognized or appreciated as equal partners in the arts, law, politics, business, religion, or sports, I gave the woman an acceptable hyperfemale, unattainable domestic challenge to channel her energy. This preoccupation is gross and perverse, and from now on I am going to direct my energies toward women's equality.

I am starting a magazine called *Phenomenal Women,* where I promise there will be no mention of diets, anything low-fat, or getting rid of cellulite. No lyposuction, no decorating, no arranging, no makeovers. I vow, in protest of this restraint, never to bake or frost another cake, and never to design or construct an appetizer tray in the shape of the Statue of Liberty. In addition, I will never participate in another project or magazine whose purpose is to have a woman be a better mother, wife, daughter, homemaker, and citizen. Instead, I will put all my extra energy into a new magazine called *Good Fathers and Husbands,* a guide for men—to get the house done, be sexy for their wives, and always cheerful for their family. In closing, with great regret and remorse, I vow never to arrange, prune, or cultivate a hydrangea. What? Me, never do anything with a hydrangea! Are you kidding? APRIL FOOL!

April To-Do List

Interview people with the name of April for my new book *In the Name of April.*

Redo entire house for a spring theme. This year tulips. Re-upholster all furniture in tulip sheets that I recycled by photographing tulips in Holland last year and then photosilkscreened the images on fabric in my silk-screening studio in South Carolina.

Recycle! Make thirty-foot outdoor robin redbreast out of old bottle caps and beer bottles. Redbreast made out of orange crush cans slightly rusted. In flashing lights next to robin in tree are the words: The early bird gets the worm.

Start feeding hybrid chickens special Gummi Bear and tutti-frutti ice cream so they will lay decorated eggs.

With my hybrid chickens — her eggs come out not just colored, dyed but designed!

Have an April showers party that takes place under a large tent that I recycled from all of the neighbors' old shower curtains. Serve hot drinks made from melted cough drops and ginger ale. Refrain from recycling cough drops.

Make collapsible bunny costume out of recycled cardboard egg cartons so it folds into purse and you can wear it at a moment's notice.

Dedicate April 5 and 12 to thinking about things to make from freeze-dried earthworms.

April 17—Walk down the aisles of Wal-Mart and feel sorry for myself because I haven't started my spring cleaning.

Spray-paint window screens lavender and yellow for something to do.

Read ancient myths about the rites of spring so it sounds like spring cleaning is more than a bottle of Pine Sol and Clorox.

Yes, even I have a mother! And thinking about a new and exciting yet homemade quality gift for Mother's Day is tension provoking. Well, let me share with you how I came upon this unusual gift to be made by your very own hands and the materials grown right from your own body! I've come to the conclusion that there is a craft project in everything around us. You just have to know how to find it!

Every time I would take a shower and I would shave my armpits and legs I would find myself looking down the drain and saying to myself, "That's wasted hair! There's a project in there somewhere." All of that hair, week after week, just going down the drain. I just had to shake my head and sigh.

Then the day after Mother's Day last year I was getting out of the tub, looking at all my hair and standing on the bathmat, and I was thinking that I had to get started on next year's gifts. When it hit me—I should make a bathmat out of my very own arm and leg hair. Presto! A great idea was born. What mother would not want a bathmat made from their very own child's hair! Come to think of it, I don't think I would want a gift like this. Well, better not take all of the blame, so I decided to make it a family project. I called all my siblings and asked them to send me their excess hair, their shaved hair, their hair left in the tub.

The process of braiding such small hairs is a snap when you use my method. I just stick all the hair in my pasta maker with a little Elmer's Glue-All, and the newly made hair pasta yarn comes out perfectly! Sometimes I spin the hair on a spinning wheel (especially

How To Make Mom a Hairbathmat

1. SHOWER + WASH

2. SHAVE PITS

3. SHAVE LEGS

4. HAIR IN DRAIN

5. THERE IS AN IDEA IN THAT TUB

6. COLLECT HAIR — HAVE SIBLINGS SAVE AND MAIL HAIR

Sis's HAIR

7.

GLUE HAIR TO JUMP ROPES AND
EXTENSION CORDS AND BRAID

8. PUT HAIR AND GLUE IN
PASTA MAKER - NO ANGEL HAIR
—please—

9.

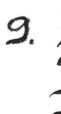

BRAID HAIR
PASTA

over →

10. You DID IT! You MADE A HAIR BATHMAT

11. With EXTRA HAIR - MAKE COASTERS

12. GIVE TO MOM FOR MOTHER'S DAY

oh, I hope it's a big b of chocolates or an azalea !!

Once your mother steps on her hair bathmat she'll slowly forget her wanting of a big bottle of perfume or taken out to dinner for Mothers Day.

if I'm demonstrating the process—it gives it that antiquey feeling). I do have a secret trick that I use when I'm feeling especially lazy that I'll share with you. I take jump ropes, electrical cords, anything else lying about the house, and dip them in glue. Then I stick my hair on it and braid!

My mother loved her hair bathmat. This year I'm doing a set of place mats. If you have any extra hair left, use for a coaster. Don't worry. You won't get any spills going through these coasters, especially if you've been using a good creme rinse.

For friends and siblings, instead of an extremely personal gift like a hair bathmat, I like to give flowers for Mother's Day. If I can't find the perfect flowers, then I just help Mother Nature herself a little and I paint the petals. I just spray-paint directly in the garden

the coaster
is made
out of what?!

WATCH OUT
FOR SPILLS
WHEN THEY
FIND OUT
THE COASTER
IS MADE OUT
OF HUMAN HAIR.

or I just paint directly on the flowers after I cut them. I believe in perfecting nature. If it's not the exact pink you want, change it. You have to let your garden know who is in control!

I give my children a bouquet of flowers on Mother's Day to remind them of all the pain I went through to have them. On each petal I'll paint scenes of having an episiotomy, my twenty hours of painful back labor, etc. I call it my bouquet of motherhood and I give it to remind them of everything I've done for them and how I've suffered for them. This keeps everyone in balance. It's hard for me to understand why everyone is not so good at painting under a high-powered magnifying glass. But if this is your case, then just sketch the birth scene on the vase. The crowning is the best.

Sometimes I write useful sayings on the petals and vase, such as "I almost died for you" or "I ruined my life for you" or, my favorite, "Your father left me after he looked at you, but I stayed."

Looking for a craft project that typifies motherhood? A project that only a new mother can do? Try a nursing painting! When I was breast-feeding my daughter, there was a lot of hoopla about body secretions and art. Like the Andres Serrano photograph of a crucifix in urine or Ron Athey blood prints. So become part of the Artworld. When you are a nursing mother take the time out to do a nursing painting. It is a nice keepsake for your child or to hang in her room. Here's how.

Nursing Painting

You will need:
Pieces of black velvet in the sizes you want your painting
The ability to lactate

Spread out the black velvet on a table. Get comfortable. Squeeze breast so milk squirts out on velvet. Make abstract design. Let dry. The imprint will be barely visible. Date, sign, and give title. When framing, do not mat. Let the velvet float without the glass touching the painting.

May Projects

Embroider the world's largest sampler with every language's word for *mother* including extinct languages and derogatory expressions. Unveil 250-foot sampler at Rockefeller Center, where Christmas tree is displayed. Have concurrent display of azalea topiaries shaped into famous mothers and objects relating to the mother.

Have rotating parties of eight coming over to try my new garlic and cashew butterscotch pie.

Nursing Painting

Have new TV show called *Dinner at My House,* where different people come over to my house for dinner and they compliment me. First-month guests: Chelsea Clinton, Ringo Starr, William Shatner, Michael Musto, Ice T, and Peggy Lee.

Publish article for *New York Times* Sunday *Magazine* food section—"May Backwards Spells Yam" with recipes on the yam.

growing, transplanting weeding, I love the smell the feel the texture the grime of dirt, the watering can in every size, the sprinkler is on but not in full sun - oh the nurseries! I LOVE NURSERIES, THE FOXGLOVE, THE DELPHINIUM, CORAL BELLS I CAN'T HAVE TOO MANY - The plant sales! A Trellis. I OWN A TRELLIS That once was in the Garden, the ROSE garden of Helen HAYES. Then there are the ROSES, the annuals to pick up color! I LIKE PETUNIAS, MORNING GLORIES, ALYSSUM, PANSIES, I just live the rest of the year for

JUNE

Wherever I go in June, the only conversation is the garden, the garden, the garden. Any amateur can pronounce gladiolus, dahlia, lilac. But can they say Iridacae, Compositae, Oleaceae? What you need to do is to learn the plants' names in Latin. Then, whenever a plant is brought up such as a sunflower, you say, "You mean the Helianthus." When tuberose comes up, you say, "Polianthes." That goes for naming your children too. Don't name your child some common name like Heather, use the name in Latin, Calluna. Using Latin demands respect. Using Latin means you are not fooling around, that you are to be taken seriously.

1. WINDOW BOX   2. STEPS   3. PORCH

find the empty spaces for more plants
TURN OVER FOR ANSWER.

1. DOUBLE WINDOW BOX 2. BOTTOM STEP 3. VINE ON PORCH RAILING.

DOUBLE WINDOW BOX. BOTTOM STEP. VINE ON PORCH

The other part of gardening that will get you noticed is volume. That means every square inch of available space needs to have a pot with a pansy, petunia, or geranium. Every windowsill, every step, every corner of the porch, every curb, needs a flowering bloom. And don't forget to have as many plants as possible hanging from the porch! Use lots and lots of moss.

Nothing gives me more satisfaction than my obsession with the growing, the pruning, the planting, the weeding, the blooming, the transplanting. I live for constant maintenance. But why stop there? Once you get started, don't stop with the obvious.

Last summer I was so into my total obsession with gardening that I just couldn't take the time out to shower for a few days. Well, maybe it was a week. Well, wouldn't you know that under my left armpit I started growing marigolds! The dwarf orange variety. I left them alone till they got established. Then I would raise my

arms while in the shower so the seedlings would just get slightly sprayed. Within a fortnight, I am happy to say, I had full blooms.

I got so excited about my personal garden that I've been experimenting with other seeds on other parts of the body. There is nothing quite as stunning, aromatic, or attractive as a tomato plant growing right out of your cleavage. Making an entrance is what the personal garden is all about.

Tired of picking the toe jam out of your toes or the lint out of your special someone's belly button? I planted an herb garden with wonderful results.

This personal garden is taken at face value (or, excuse me, body value). The body garden is wonderful to have; you can take your garden with you! For those of you who don't have any outdoor area, the body garden is a perfect solution.

If your figure can't handle the beefsteak variety try a cherry tomato

Try growing a little rosemary by The BIG TOE

Father's Day

June also means Father's Day. What am I making Dad for Father's Day? Last year I made a BBQ sauce torte. I buy every kind of BBQ sauce that I can find and then I spread or pour the entire bottle between slices of bread. I'll start with an entire rosemary focaccia topped with smoky BBQ sauce, then 6–8 bagels (any kind will do except the cinnamon raisin) topped with a salsa BBQ, then 7-grain bread with red cayenne BBQ, then pumpernickel and cilantro bread topped with molasses BBQ, then 12 individual sponge cakes topped with mustard chutney BBQ, then sourdough rye topped with 4-alarm BBQ, then small individual ladyfingers with Cajun BBQ. Slice it and it will serve 6.

Now, if you are planning to serve your BBQ torte and are looking for a theme for your Father's Day party that will guarantee you will hear shrieks from your guests, I suggest a party inspired by Lorena and John Wayne Bobbitt. The phallus can be a colorful and complicated subject for the dad day. Just give me any excuse to make sausage!

Once I start making sausage, I can't stop. I'll go for days. I have my very own sausage workshop with specific sausage grinders, choppers, and casing stretchers. Of course, food is the most essential part of a successful party. Bratwurst, bockwurst, kielbasa, smoky links, all just the right length, just the right thickness.

Of course, a party is not considered a real success unless the table has a memorable centerpiece. For my centerpiece I carved Oscar Mayer hot dogs into the shape of penises and I put them in old mason jars that I've filled with water and food coloring. I put different size jars filled with the penis/hot dogs in the middle of the table and add a few candles for accent. I find that the mason jars look best when there's a little bit of rust on the lid and the candle wax drips down the sides.

Looking for conversation? You're not going to have a quiet time with this centerpiece! I get to feel very Freudian when my guests come up to me and ask, "Karen, what is in those jars?" and I answer, "What do you think is in those jars?" The one thing that everyone agrees on is that you'll never see these for sale in the Eddie Bauer home catalogue. Well, maybe *my* catalogue.

For party games, instead of playing pin the tail on the donkey, we play pin the sausage on the man. When the party goes on and you want your guests to leave, give them each half a sausage, send them over to the 7 Eleven parking lot, and see who can throw it the farthest.

June Recycling

Don't know what to do with those spots on your husband's or wife's ties? I collect all the stained ties. I save all of my finger- and toenail clippings. The nails can be polished or unpolished or even fake, but I prefer nails that are painted. Painted nails are like works of art with things like the American flag on them or sayings like "Have a nice day." I Super-Glue these

CAJUN BBQ SAUCE

4 ALARM BBQ SAUCE

MUSTARD CHUTNEY BBQ SAUCE

MOLASSES BBQ SAUCE

RED CAYENNE BBQ SAUCE

CHUNKY SALSA BBQ SAUCE

SMOKEY BBQ SAUCE

DAD THING!

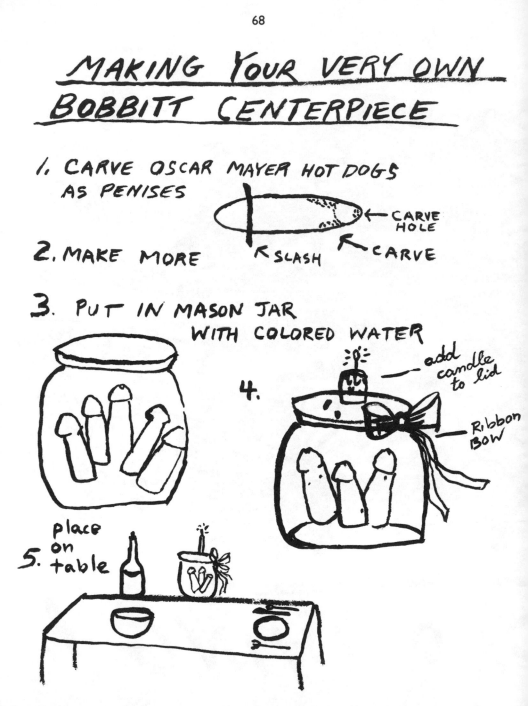

MAKING YOUR VERY OWN BOBBITT CENTERPIECE

1. CARVE OSCAR MAYER HOT DOGS AS PENISES

← CARVE HOLE

← SLASH

← CARVE

2. MAKE MORE

3. PUT IN MASON JAR WITH COLORED WATER

4.

add candle to lid

Ribbon Bow

5. place on table

USING YOUR Electronic EQUIPMENT

WITH THE BOBBITTS

1. TAPE RECORDER

MAKE A VOICE LOOP OF LORENA WHEN SHE WAS ON THE STAND. COMBINE W/ **REALM** OF SENSES.

2. VIDEO

A. VIDEO EDITS OF NEWSCASTER SAYING "PENIS"

B. INTERVIEW **OTHER** LORENAS ON WHAT IT IS LIKE TO BE NAMED LORENA

C. DO A VIDEO **REENACTMENT** OF LORENA HOLDING PENIS + THROWING IT AWAY

3. DO COMPUTER DRAWING OF JOHN'S REATTACHED PENIS

yes, that spells Crumb Buns!

nails to the tie in a mosaic pattern. On one tie I'll do a pattern of his astrological sign or on another I'll do the male symbol. Some-times I'll write his favorite sayings like "Heck" or "Crumb Buns."

June Gardening Planner

Divide garden into the design of the seven continents and begin collecting the manure of the animals from the continents by travel and mail and place the different manures in the different gardens. Begin a catalogue company of exotic and endangered animals' manure to display in the garden as fertilizer and as temporary decorative purposes. Have an infomercial where viewers can see for themselves the different sculptural properties of manure. Manure as art supply. Using manure as a material like clay, I will demonstrate how you can make an entire set of Beatrix Potter's woodland creatures and farm animals with only one cow pile. And it's biodegradable!

A Typical Gardening Day in June

4:00 A.M.—Wake up with nightmares that a fungus has already taken up the rosebush.

4:30 A.M.—Can't get back to sleep. Get flashlight and go out to examine the leaves of the rose. Don't make it. Discover deer ate last of tulips.

5:15 A.M.—Begin plans to build fortress around the entire garden to keep all animals away.

7:00 A.M.—Construction crew arrives to begin 15-foot brick wall around garden.

7:30 A.M.—Discover that my copper thread gardening gloves are turning my hands green.

8:00 A.M.—Stung by entire hive of yellow jackets while disturbing their nest while chopping down a dead dogwood. Hospitalization required. Allergic reaction.

Three days later

7:00 A.M.—Wake up. Depressed because I cannot see garden from window, only brick wall.

7:30 A.M.—Entire crew arrives to take down brick wall and put up glass brick wall.

9:00 A.M.—Need to see psychiatrist about my irrational need to train plants. My need to prune, pinch, and control the way a plant grows. Special concern given to my need to force plants to grow out of their natural habitat and my mastery over their lives.

11:00 A.M.—Go to a nursery and get out of there spending only this month's rent. Begonias, pansies, alyssum.

Noon—Go to a new nursery just a little bit out of my way and spend this month's car payment on a new tiller and 4 pairs of gardening gloves.

1:30 P.M.—Go to meet a friend for lunch, but first stop at the greenhouse by their house and pick up fertilizer, lime, a garden gnome, and a St. Francis of Assisi.

2:45 P.M.—My friend, upset with me for being late for lunch, says my gardening is interfering with our friendship. She thinks gardening has overtaken my life.

4:00 P.M.—Instead of going home, I first stop at a little out-of-the-way place to pick up some coleus and impatiens even though I just bought some last week. I just couldn't stop myself.

5:30 P.M.—Instead of making dinner, I plant my new specimens.

7:15 P.M.—Friends and family over when I get inside. A gardener I know from a couple of years back is over too. I'll talk for a few minutes, then I'll get back to the garden.

7:30 P.M.—Just when I say I'm going back out to the garden they close the door. My family and friends confront me on my addiction to the garden. They say I've lost control and that I need to start going to Gardening Anonymous meetings. The gardener I used to know says she'll take me. Or, it was talked about maybe to go to a rehab center. I run out of the house and go to the garden, pulling out weeds. This is going to be very hard.

2:00 A.M.—I sneak out of the house and go to an all-night super-market and check out their display of plants. I plan to buy just one plant, but then I go back into the store till all the plants are bought. I drive 50 miles to the next 24-hour supermarket to buy baby tomato plants and some of last month's azaleas. This is pathetic. Gardening has taken over my life. But I can't help myself. Then I return home and with a flashlight between my teeth, I'm planting and digging in the middle of the night.

7:00 A.M.—My family finds me collapsed in the pansy patch. This is where I bottomed out. From now on it's one day at a time.

THE PRESCRIBED LIVING IT UP METHOD OF DIRECT SPEECH TOWARDS MOWING THE LAWN

1. HONEY, COULD YOU MOW THE LAWN?

2. HONEY, COULD YOU, WOULD YOU WITH SUGAR ON TOP MOW THE LAWN?

3. DARLING, SPOT'S BALL IS LOST IN THE GRASS!

4. Sweetheart, SPOT IS LOST IN THE GRASS!

5. HONEY, THE KIDS ARE LOST IN THE GRASS!

6. MOW THE DAMN LAWN FOR GOD'S SAKE!

The Month of Grass

IF YOU DON'T HAVE GRASS YOU DON'T HAVE A LIFE

After the garden, then there is the grass! Grass is a whole science unto itself. TEXTURE, LENGTH, COLOR, DANDELIONS, MOWING, THATCHING. Your spouse's summer should revolve around grass. Remember, you do not have a successful marriage if your spouse is not preoccupied with the grass. If it's July and he hasn't developed an avid interest in the grass, you know your relationship is on the rocks. START COUNSELING IMMEDIATELY OR FIND A GOOD ATTORNEY!

These are some measures that can be taken to try to entice your spouse into the world of GRASS.

Buy a new lawn mower. All men love gadgets. Buy the most expensive, loudest, biggest, reddest lawn mower. Sometimes losing interest in grass can be a sign of a midlife crisis. Men at this time

OCCASIONALLY   NEVER   YES!

want to buy a new motorcycle or sports car. Start with a new hot rod, ride-on lawn mower.

Tell him he's sexy when he's sweating.

Invite men over who are obsessed with grass.

Go over to people's houses where the grass is taken care of immaculately with avid attention to detail, never letting a strand get too tall or scraggly.

Start telling dog owners that it's perfectly all right for dogs to use your lawn as a toilet.

Start having the kids say they are embarrassed to live in the neighborhood because the grass is so yellow.

Say "I love to make love to the smell of newly cut grass."

Make a tape and play it while he is sleeping, saying, "I love to cut grass. I love to cut grass. I love to cut grass."

Ask neighbors to whis-

There GOES THE NEIGHBORHOOD. THEY SEEMED SO RESPONSIBLE. You'D NEVER KNOW BY THE LOOKS OF THEM THAT THEY'D NEGLECT THEIR GRASS. KIDS, WHY DON'T YoU GO TO someone elses House **to play?** I DON'T WANT YOU TO PICK UP ANY BAD HABITS. You'LL HAVE YOUR OWN HOUSE ONE DAY. Oh, my GOD, that GRASS IS ACTUALLY GoING To SEED. There's A FAMILY OF RABBITS LIVING IN THAT LAWN. GOD, I CAN'T WAIT TILL WINTER + SNOW So I WON'T **have**

to look at   that eyesore.

I DON'T CARE   IF IT'S NATURE

I DON'T LIKE IT.

I LIKE MY GRASS   LIKE MONEY, GREEN.

per loudly, "What has happened to their grass? They used to be such nice people."

Send anonymous letters—The status of your reputation in the neighborhood is at stake. I suggest you immediately seek help for the neglect of the care of your lawn.

If you have no space outdoors (say you live in some crummy little studio apartment in some high-rise building) then you need to bring the lawn inside and make a grass room. I grow grass, dandelions and all, right on my walls. Yes, mowing it is a problem, but it's better than when I had it growing on the floor and dogs would think that they were outside. I used to hand out Baggies to the dogs' owners.

For this project you will first need to line the wall with a base of plastic coating. I have found that the cheapest and easiest way is to recycle the plastic grocery bags and those plastic bags that the newspaper comes in every morning. You get your hot-glue gun out and make a quilt of those bags that is the size of the wall that you are using. Next, you Krazy-Glue the quilt to the wall. Now, this plastic shield might seem like a little bit too much work, but it will prevent water and earthworms from invading your next-door neighbor's apartment and avoiding that lawsuit will be well worth the time invested. Take it from someone who knows.

You next attach chicken wire to the wall using nails or a staple gun. You then add moss to the wall. Last you throw on seeds and remember to water well every day until you see the thick, green results.

1. Attach plastic BAGS TO WALL USING HOT GLUE GUN. HOT GLUE BAGS TO EACH OTHER FIRST TO MAKE QUILT

2. HAMMER CHICKEN WIRE OVER BAGS

3. STICK IN MOSS SO YOU CAN'T SEE WIRE OR PLASTIC

4. THROW ON SEEDS

5 WATER DAILY

6. ENJOY YOUR GRASS WALL

Of course, if you want immediate gratification, you should sod the walls. Once I said to myself, "Karen, I just can't find the color green that I want to paint my walls. I want a green like that of Kentucky bluegrass." So I went and dug up the bluegrass in the exact color that I wanted and stuck it up on my walls.

I was looking at my Chia Pet when it hit me—why should I stop there? Why should I stop with a little ceramic pig or dog? I started growing sprouts on my overstuffed chair. Take your stuffed, ragged chair and soak it with water, sprinkle with alfalfa seeds, and in a couple of days you've got a sprouted chair.

Not only is the sprouted chair comfortable, it is practical too. When the ladies are over for lunch, they always like to cut their own sprouts for salads and sandwiches. Your chair has never been so yummy.

grass chair

July Recycling

I hope you are collecting those Popsicle sticks! You never know when you just might need them for making lamps, making your patio deck, or just making your own Popsicles.

Fourth of July

The problems of our country could be solved by changing the colors of our flag. How about mauve, beige, and gray? "Who can make a dessert out of those colors?" you ask. Okay, so I'll be laughed out of every women's magazine. But you aren't going to laugh when you hear these flag colors I propose—shocking pink, electric blue, lime green, and Day-glo yellow. Just imagine the Jell-O desserts that will come out of that color combination.

Now, you are thinking, that's four colors. That's right. Why do we have to have only three colors? The colors and design of the flag should change on an annual basis, and be decided by a professional academy. In following years there could be stained glass, kaleidoscope, and paisley patterns. For the first year I propose that the design of the flag should be America's to-do list that can be checked off with each task completed.

After the first year, with my design, we will open up the competition. As a nation, we can be very creative with who can design the flag. We can charge a lot of money to companies who want to design the flag with their logo such as McDonald's, Pepsi, Fritos, Budweiser, and Microsoft, to help with our national debt. I think people from around the world would certainly recognize our flag if they saw a giant hamburger on it!

There could also be a giant lottery to create a new flag. Citizens could buy tickets. In order to make more money and have more variety, we could open up the competition to the whole world. Then on July Fourth one ticket would be drawn. The winner could have her face on the flag or a child could pose with Barney, a Disney character, or a pack of cigarettes, so the country could get some cash for the endorsement. Or the winner could paint, design, or write a poem for the flag.

Having the design of the flag change every year is going to be great for the furnishing, clothing, and decorating industries. Every year people will have to buy a new flag, a new flag tablecloth, a new flag sweatshirt, etc. Just imagine the food magazines. There will have to be new desserts and menus to correlate with the flag. I think I'm getting excited about the possibilities.

A lot of discussion has taken place about the burning of the flag. I suggest that the flag should be made so it can't be burned. All flags should be made out of stainless steel. Wouldn't that be great for the steel industry! The only problem I see is in waving the flags. Even if there is a design of a flag on a sweatshirt, it has to be made out of tin so it can't be burned. Yes, flags will be heavy but they won't burn. Can't our government make a flag that won't burn?

Well, we don't have the flag colors changed yet, so I've got to do the best I can with red, white, and blue.

Blueberry pancake breakfast with strawberry sauce and whipped cream for 15,000 in my front yard for friends and family. Next year I just might be handing out 15,000 to-do-list flags with a hydrangea in the middle made out of cast iron.

Now, having 15,000 is just a little too much for my guest toilet, so I have to bring out the Porta Pottis. I've always had a problem with the soft toilet seats. I always feel like I'm sitting on someone's tummy or big behind. Mr. Rush Limbaugh has always put himself in the position of having all the answers for the country and that he is the most patriotic, so I thought it appropriate to put his image on the throne on our nation's birthday. I've made a true-to-life stuffed-bean-bag toilet seat of Rush Limbaugh. The male when urinating merely immerses himself in the soft arms of Rush and urinates. For the number-two act, the guest leans back on the bean-bag toilet seat of Rush and eliminates. You'll be sure to find the Rush seat the most comfortable toilet seat you have ever sat in.

I know that July Fourth is Independence Day, but I actually like to celebrate Dependence Day. So after the pancake breakfast we participate in the Dependence Day parade. We all enter the parade with the objects that we are dependent on. We have floats dedicated to the curling iron, the golf club, the microwave oven, permanent press, or fat-free ice cream.

At the parade I gave my annual domestic address. Now everyone is always talking about cutting domestic spending. Well, the problem is we never have had the true sense of the words domestic spending. I propose that people are allocated a certain amount of money and they can buy whatever they need for their domestic purposes. We should make sure that every family has a decent corkscrew. I'm sure you've brought a bottle of wine to your hostess's home and looked at the opener they gave you and you just thought, "This opener is a piece of crap." Everyone would feel better if they had new washcloths or a grapefruit spoon. Everyone would feel better if they had an object they could depend on. That is what real America is about, discovering new objects to buy, cherish, and create time, energy, or a project around!

AUGUST

It's hot and humid but you have to do it anyway. August means it's time to paint the outside of the house. When you hear my method, you won't want to put it off another year.

There is nothing as boring, as provincial, as statementless as a solidly painted house. It's always a white house, a blue house, a beige house. Even when the colors are stronger and bolder and brighter, all the house really ever gets thought of as is THAT HOT-PINK HOUSE WITH THE ELECTRIC-BLUE TRIM AND THE LIME-GREEN DOOR. That's not very nice. That's not a classic.

One reason I've put off painting my house is that you have to get out the ladders, the scaffolding, the paint trays, the paintbrushes, the painting outfit I hate, the paint rags, the cleanup. Can you imagine painting your house without washing a brush? Well, you'd better believe it when you use my method.

Painting is an art form, so why not look at our houses as works of art, big canvases. I've been inspired by Jackson Pollock to creating both the Splash House and the Drip House.

The Splash House

You will need:

500 assorted sizes of balloons

Enough paint in different colors—quarts are easiest to pour from

Kids or adults for a collaborative work, or you can do it yourself for an individual work of artistic expression.

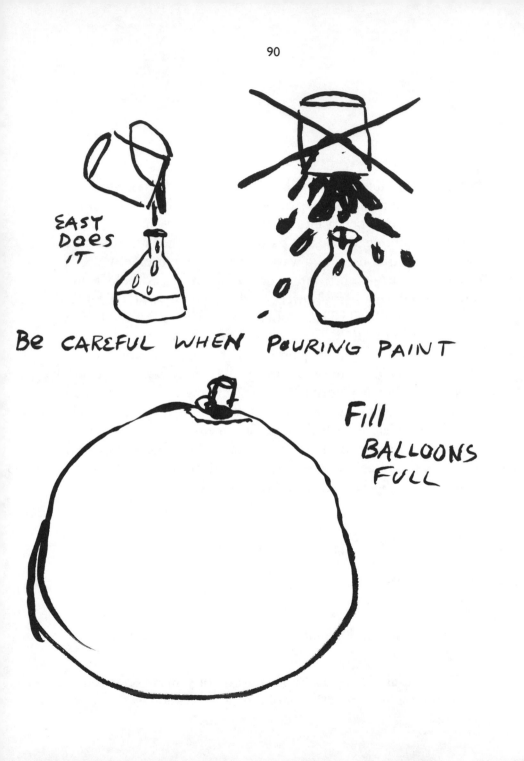

if you don't fill Balloon enough— IT WILL Roll off HOUSE AND COULD BREAK ON YOU!

Select a balloon. Select a color. Pour paint into balloons. You can either pour paint into the balloons one at a time or get a whole palette system going with lots of balloons. I prefer to do a little of both. I fill up a variety of colors so I can really go at it. Fill the bal-

splatter
House

loons very full. They will break more easily. There is nothing more frustrating than having the balloon come back at you and pop. Tie balloon. Pick up balloon and begin to throw at house. Throw the balloon quickly and furiously for the best splatter result. Get into some system. Start from the middle, start from the sides, the bottom, or top. Get into a frenzy. Change colors. No matter what, don't stop. The beauty is in the constant action. Do not answer phones. Do not go inside. If you don't like the color or splatter, go to another area or side of the house and come back. Do all four sides of house, moving your setup as you change. I find it is too distracting to work on all four sides at the same time, but you can if you want the four sides similar. When splatter-painting the door, try not to use smaller balloons. It looks corny, affected, or on purpose.

The Drip House

What you will need:

One gallon of paint for every 12 to 18 inches of width of side of house. This is for a 2- to 3-story house. Use one quart for 8 to 12 inches for one-story house.

Access to roof.

Buy paint in variety of colors. You need to buy more than two colors to see the drips. Bring paint up to roof and remove gutters. Line paint cans up on edge of roof. Quickly turn paint can to its side so paint drips out and to side of house. While paint is dripping down side of house, move on to next can. You are finished when all cans are overturned.

Painting the door. Now, you can do a smaller version of the drip house for the front door. Simply put paint in paper cups and line up on top of the door when door is open. Let the paint drip down the door.

Now, I know some of you are worrying about the windows. That the windows are going to get paint on them. Yes, you are going to get some paint on your windows. In fact, you are going to get a lot of paint on your windows. Big deal. You're complaining about a little thing like not being able to see out of your windows! Well, good art needs to be sacrificed for, and if you want to graduate from the occasional hobbyist, then you need to be willing to sacrifice a little sunlight for your project.

Drying time six to eight weeks for both designs.

August is also the month for some time off, the vacation. The proper way to have a vacation is to ensure that you do as much as possible. I know I've had a great vacation when I'm so exhausted that I'm ready for another vacation.

YOU'll NEVER HAVE seen ANYTHING LIKE IT

drip house

When I decide on a vacation, I insist on going somewhere where there are lots and lots of lines at the restaurants, getting a newspaper, a parking space. Waiting means that I am in a popular place. Who wants to go on vacation out-of-the-way? I certainly don't. If you can, get a summer house. There is nothing better than to have another house to clean, decorate, and buy for. Before I had my summer house I felt that I could have a handle on things. Now it is impossible. There is so much to do. I'm the most relaxed when I have more and more projects ahead of me. I have found my true real self. Buying in doubles is so much fun.

August Recycling

Have you ever gone to the beach and found plastic tampon inserters lying around on the sand or floating in the water? Believe me, there's a project in there! Well, I have the sewing project for you without sewing. Take an old bathing suit that still fits and hot-glue the tampon containers to the suits. They are a little uncomfortable for sitting in, but they are great for swimming in.

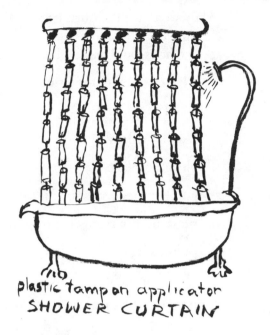

plastic tampon applicator
SHOWER CURTAIN

Another fun, useful project is the revival of the beaded curtain, but using the found plastic tampons. Or they make a great shower curtain, but make sure still to use a liner.

A Day in August

6:00 A.M.—Wake up house guests for BBQ breakfast of quail eggs benedict with hollandaise sauce coated with Cocoa Puffs and grilled using mesquite wood.

6:15 A.M.—Guests won't wake up. What do they think this is, some kind of rest camp? Start banging pots and pans and turn on AC/DC real loud.

6:30 A.M.—They're up with some lame excuse that their body is tired from chopping the cord of wood yesterday that I made them do before they could eat dinner.

They won't eat the quail eggs benedict. They just want some toast and a pot of coffee. I give them a list of the chores to do around the house and garden before they can take their shower.

List of chores for guests:

weed

feed baby lamb

clean fireplace

gather blueberries for pies for dinner

make herb wreaths for neighbors

polish silver

clean barbecue

10:00 A.M.—While they are in the shower, drive thirty-five miles to get the best smoked oysters for cocktails. While driving, have panic attack because there is nothing to do tomorrow. Eat the three pounds of smoked oysters on the way home. When halfway home, turn around to buy three more pounds of smoked oysters.

11:00 A.M.—Go to beach. Start roasting the pig. Dig a pit to fire our clay coffee mugs with designs of beach scenes.

Noon—Show kids what a real sand castle looks like by bringing out the architectural plans for Buckingham Palace with my own improvements.

12:30 P.M.—Set the most beautiful picnic. First a basket made from braided dried hydrangea and porcelain berries, fishing lines and discarded hairnets (found in the garbage of the local clam shack). A tablecloth made from sewing old bathing suits. Cover the suits with Scotch tape for quick cleanups. Glasses made by hand-cutting found bottles washed onto the shore. Plates made from ground shells and seaweed imprints. Napkins are made from birch bark. Place mats decorated with handwritten personal horror stories of being sunburnt. I demonstrate the making of the entire picnic basket collection on the beach with hundreds of onlookers for my new book— *Making the Picnic As Precious and Time-Consuming As Possible.* OOPS, I forgot to pack a picnic lunch. Well, it's all in the process, isn't it? We will just have to wait for the suckling pig.

3:00 P.M.—Time for my annual kite-making contest. I enter a kite of a giant rat, made from gum wrappers, with a background of the Sistine Chapel, made from cigarette cellophane wrappers that are hand-colored in nonwashable Magic Markers. The only problem is that you can't make out that Sistine Chapel in the sky, but you sure can make out that rat. I gave first prize to a kite with the blown-up imprints of my feet smashing grapes and my hands using a hot-glue gun with the phrase Every moment is a craft moment.

4:00 P.M.—Suckling pig explodes. I hate this damn month. I need a holiday. There is no holiday in this month, so I think it is time I give this month some holiday ideas. August needs a national holiday!

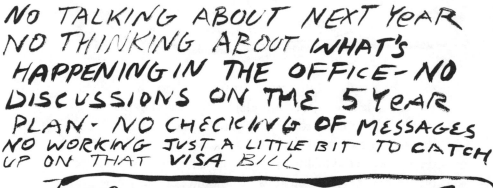

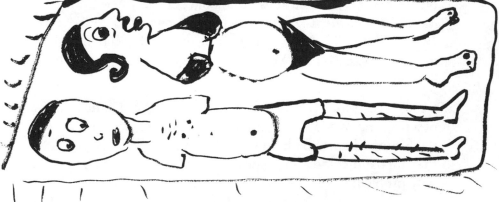

August 1—Naked Truth Day

On this first day of the hottest day of the month it is allowed that people appear nude in public. People can appear in restaurants, walking their dogs, in line in the post office, nude. People at their jobs can also be nude, including all civil workers, like postal carriers. Policemen and -women can be nude, but fire personnel are exempt from this Naked Truth Day custom.

Naked Truth Day begins with the president and his wife greeting the public nude on the lawn while a rooster crows. The rooster is given food. If the rooster crows before eating the food, it is going to be a hot August. If the rooster eats before he crows, it is going to be a mild August. Children pretend they are roosters. Across the land there are cock-a-doodle-doo contests. Generally people sit around drinking beer nude and watching a game of baseball played in the nude.

On this day everyone has to tell the truth no matter how painful, and that is where the fun begins. People are allowed to ask whatever they want as long as they are willing to suffer the consequences of hearing the truth. There are no excuses, only the truth. Because the truth has to be told, Washington is closed for the day. All politicians are in seclusion. Rush Limbaugh takes the day off, too, but not his clothes.

September

I look forward to Labor Day! I always plan a party with the real, true meaning of labor. Labor pains.

I throw a party with the idea of celebrating and illuminating women giving birth, as opposed to men giving birth. Yes, I know there is Mother's Day, but this is the celebration of the labor of birth and I want it a national holiday. Ever since Arnold Schwarzenegger made a film implying that he could have a baby better than me I've wanted to have this party.

I always have the labor party outside and inside. In every room I have videos of live births. Have the neighbors and guests bring their birth tape or borrow one from the library or a birthing center. Outside, I have projected on the side of my house slides of birthing scenes, including cesareans. Then in quadraphonic sound we hear the women, loud and clear, giving birth. The screams and cries. Yes, this is Labor Day.

About a month before the party I borrow my neighbor's birth photos and I blow them up and make place mats or print on coffee mugs.

Later, with dessert, I show tapes of episiotomies.

Back to School

September means back to school and it means gathering up all the devices necessary to ensure that your child is not viewed as an ordi-

CATERED SCHOOL LUNCH

1ST COURSE
- ICE WATER (SPRING) WITH Fresh lemon
- SOUP- MUSHROOM CONSOMMÉ WITH WAGON WHEEL PASTA

2ND COURSE
- HAWAIIAN PUNCH
- SALAD WITH PAUL NEWMAN'S DRESSING

3RD COURSE-
- ORGANIC COCA COLA SERVED OVER MINT ICE
- CHICAGO STYLE THINCRUST PIZZA WITH THAI NOODLES AND COCKTAIL WEINERS

4TH COURSE
- HÄAGEN DAZS ICE CREAM BAR SERVED ON WEDGWOOD

nary student. You're wondering how you can give your child that certain edge over other children. You've bought the designer clothes and school bags. You've signed them up to all the appropriate social climbing extracurricular activities. But are you forgetting something? We need to fill all the moments in a child's life. A moment that is usually not given much attention is the school lunch. This is an important peer activity that requires great skill and guidance on your part to make sure that your child assumes a position of leadership when sitting at the lunch table.

Now, I know that you have made the mandatory lunches from the pages of my book *Gourmet School Lunches.* So many of you have written me to tell me that your child never ate peanut butter until you started growing your own peanuts, at my suggestion. Now try this. This year I made a special trip to the Amazon, where I have invested in a Brazil nut plantation with a group of other parents. I travel to my plantation and hand-select the Brazil nuts that I later make into Brazil butter. This is an example of parents at work for the vital interest of their children. The children haven't yet liked the Brazil butter, but it was worth the trip and it is good to expose your child to different tastes whether they like them or not.

There are three approaches to this vital meal. One is making the lunch yourself, two is taking over the school lunch program and designing the menu, and finally, having your child's lunch be catered or hand-delivered.

WRAPPING THE SCHOOL LUNCH

Have you been spending hours and hours preparing your child's lunch, then merely wrapping that sandwich in pathetic, ordinary waxed paper? If you have, you aren't giving your child the fulfillment from his peers at that moment. Yes, you are forgetting

if that's what his sandwich wrap looks like imagine his underwear!

something. You can make something out of that important transitory moment, that powerful, tension-provoking moment of what is in the sandwich bag. Don't ever let your child go to school with ordinary waxed paper wrapping his roasted eggplant, goat cheese, and red pepper baguette!

Take two pieces of waxed paper. Put shaved crayon in between the paper. Iron the waxed paper with the crayon shavings. The crayons melt into a multitude of rainbows. While still warm, wrap the sandwich. *Voilà!*

I have recorded on microcassette drum rolls from my local fireman's parade. Then I insert the computer chip into the sandwich bag, so when the sandwich is taken out of the bag, it turns on. You will need a little help from an electronics studio, but it is worth the extra money.

I also hand-crochet the bags for my child's sandwiches. Yes, it does take extra time to wash, dry, starch, and iron each lacy creation after each meal, but it's paid for by the expressions my child receives from the startled teachers.

BANANAS IN jean wrap

I've received more calls from parents, saying, "What the hell are you doing crocheting sandwich bags? Now my kid wants one." That is just the kind of response and attention I crave and work for.

I don't know what they are complaining about though, 'cause if they don't know how to knit or crochet or don't have the time, they can always fly to Brussels off-season and pick up some Belgian lace remnants. The price is best just before and after tourist season. Or buy some Belgian lace hankies and sew two together. I provide shortcuts.

I also like to make interesting wrappings for the other articles of food. For cookies I make drawstring quilt bags with the phrases "All Mine" or "I Don't Share" on them.

Bananas are whimsical characters to wrap. I make a pair of bell bottoms from an old pair of jeans which I then embroider. I stick a banana in each leg of the jeans. On each banana I draw a little face with ink that I make from wild blueberries from my yard and cream of tartar. As the jeans wear out, patch with scraps of velvet and brocades. Don't bother putting a zipper on those jeans. A quarter of an inch elastic waistband will do. And don't worry, your child will never be a second banana! That second banana goes to a friend!

Redecorating

Gee, what do you say when our teenage children tell us, "I wish you were dead!"? I say, "It's time to redecorate your room!" and my favorite theme du jour for redecorating a teenager's room is the Menendez brothers.

I've always loved the name Menendez. When I first heard it, I said to myself, "That name has such potential, such design quality," and that translates into only one thing—curtains. I love to rearrange the letters in the name, print them on sheets, and then swag the sheets over the window. I cut a letter in ??? in an organic russet potato (from my own garden) and start printing, using

MAKE IT MENENDEZ

1. DRAPERIES + SPREADS

PRINT MENENDEZ
ON **FABRICS**

PLAY WITH THE
LETTERS—

MEN
END
E
Z   MAKE IT
          CONCEPTUAL!

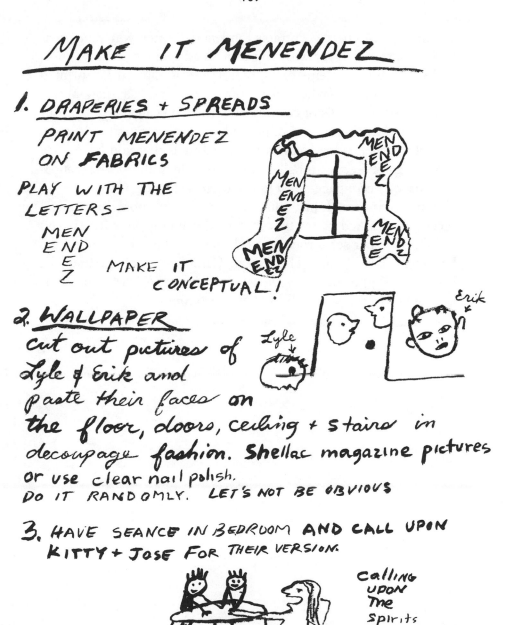

2. WALLPAPER

cut out pictures of
Lyle & Erik and
paste their faces on
the floor, doors, ceiling + stairs in
decoupage fashion. Shellac magazine pictures
or use clear nail polish.
DO IT RANDOMLY.   LET'S NOT BE OBVIOUS

3. HAVE SEANCE IN BEDROOM AND CALL UPON KITTY + JOSE FOR THEIR VERSION.

Calling
UPON
The
Spirits
of KITTY + JOSE

acrylic paint, onto the curtains, and *voilà!* After you redo their bedroom, they'll never wish you were dead again.

Every teenage friend of my children's admires these printed Menendez curtains when they come over, and it's such a nice change from footballs or cowboy patterns. You can also make your own Menendez wallpaper to go with your new curtains. Just cut out all the Menendez faces from the tabloids that you have lying around, color-Xerox and glue them onto the wall just like wallpaper. Maybe decoupage a few to the dresser drawers too.

I must confess, I just can't get enough of those brothers. I recently was asked by my best girlfriend from my New Jersey days to help style her son's rock and roll band. I started by calling the band the Lyle Look. They wear Catholic-school sweaters of maroon and gray and they even wear toupees! Wonderful. Their first song was called "I Fill My Father's Shoes."

life size
ghost
pancakes

Let's go Pumpkin

Pumpkin BREAD **Pumpkin** MUFFINS **Pumpkin** PIE
Pumpkin SOUP **Pumpkin** SOUFFLÉ **Pumpkin** CONSOMMÉ
Pumpkin CASSEROLE **Pumpkin** OMELET **Pumpkin** PANCAKES
Pumpkin BUTTER **Pumpkin** PRESERVES **Pumpkin** ICE CREAM
Pumpkin CANDY MASHED **Pumpkin** BAKED **Pumpkin**
BOILED **Pumpkin** BROILED **Pumpkin** BLANCHED **Pumpkin**
SAUTÉED **Pumpkin** STEAMED **Pumpkin** **Pumpkin** LOAF
Pumpkin MEAT LOAF **Pumpkin** EGGNOG ROASTED **Pumpkin**
STUFFED **Pumpkin** **Pumpkin** STUFFING PICKLED **Pumpkin**
DEVILED EGGS FILLED WITH **Pumpkin** **Pumpkin** SALAD
GRATED **Pumpkin** AND CARROT SALAD WITH RAISINS AND GINGER
Pumpkin CURRY **Pumpkin** OVER RICE **Pumpkin** S'MORES
Pumpkin CANAPÉS **Pumpkin** AND CHEDDAR SPREAD
Pumpkin AND GARLIC KABOBS **Pumpkin** BURGERS **Pumpkin**
FRIES **Pumpkin** MAYONNAISE **Pumpkin** DRESSING **Pumpkin**
SAUCE **Pumpkin** CIDER **Pumpkin** AND FENNEL TEA
Pumpkin CHICKEN SALAD **Pumpkin** GUACAMOLE **Pumpkin**
PUDDING **Pumpkin** JELL-O **Pumpkin** FROSTING **Pumpkin**
ICING **Pumpkin** FROSTING **Pumpkin** CREAM CHEESE FROSTING
Pumpkin WHIPPED CREAM **Pumpkin**, BEAN, AND BEEF BURRITO
Pumpkin ECLAIRS **Pumpkin** CHOP SUEY **Pumpkin** PASTA
Pumpkin PESTO **Pumpkin** MARINARA SAUCE OVER ANGEL HAIR
Pumpkin PASTA **Pumpkin** TOFU **Pumpkin** YOGURT
Pumpkin BISCUITS **Pumpkin** PIZZA DEEP-FRIED **Pumpkin**
Pumpkin LASAGNA **Pumpkin** TAMARI **Pumpkin** COFFEE
CAKE **Pumpkin** SHAKES **Pumpkin** DONUTS ROASTED
Pumpkin SEEDS **Pumpkin** GNOCCHI **Pumpkin** AND CHICKEN
POT PIE **Pumpkin** COUSCOUS **Pumpkin** FRAPPE **Pumpkin** À
LA KING GRILLED **Pumpkin** **Pumpkin** ICED TEA **Pumpkin**
JAMBALAYA **Pumpkin** CHILI **Pumpkin** COOKIES **Pumpkin**
PUDDING **Pumpkin** PARMIGIANA **Pumpkin** TORTE **Pumpkin**
CUSTARD **Pumpkin** RAVIOLI **Pumpkin** GUMMI BEARS
Pumpkin DUMPLINGS **Pumpkin** ANGEL FOOD CAKE

Pumpkin GRAVY   **Pumpkin** HOLLANDAISE   **Pumpkin** BARBE-
CUE SAUCE   **Pumpkin** SALSA   **Pumpkin** AND CORN BREAD
STUFFING   **Pumpkin** BAKED BEANS   **Pumpkin** BAKLAVA
Pumpkin BISCUITS   **Pumpkin** STUFFED CABBAGE   **Pumpkin**
EGG FOO YUNG   **Pumpkin** EGG ROLLS   **Pumpkin** ENCHILADAS
PICKLED **Pumpkin**   **Pumpkin** POPOVERS   **Pumpkin** POPCORN
Pumpkin BAKED ALASKA   **Pumpkin** LOUIS   **Pumpkin** TACOS
SUN-DRIED **Pumpkin**S   **Pumpkin** BRUSCHETTA   **Pumpkin**
POLENTA   **Pumpkin** RISOTTO   **Pumpkin** RICE BALLS
Pumpkin BISCOTTI   **Pumpkin** FRITTATA   **Pumpkin** TIRAMISU
Pumpkin SAUSAGE   **Pumpkin**-STUFFED ACORN SQUASH   ANGEL
HAIR PASTA WITH BRIE AND **Pumpkin** SAUCE   STIR-FRIED
Pumpkin   **Pumpkin** IN BALSAMIC VINEGAR   **Pumpkin** CHOP
SUEY   TEX-MEX **Pumpkin**   **Pumpkin** NIÇOISE   **Pumpkin** CAC-
CIATORE   **Pumpkin** FONDUE   EASY **Pumpkin** CASSOULET   THAI
Pumpkin   **Pumpkin** STROGANOFF   SMOKED **Pumpkin** WITH
WALNUTS AND GORGONZOLA   **Pumpkin** SCALLOPINI   SZECHUAN
Pumpkin   **Pumpkin** RELLENOS   **Pumpkin**-CRUSTED FISH
STICKS   MACARONI AND **Pumpkin**   **Pumpkin** SLOPPY JOES   MY
FAVORITE **Pumpkin** QUICHE   **Pumpkin** RATATOUILLE
PumpkinSCHNITZEL   **Pumpkin** ROULADEN   **Pumpkin** MATZO
BALL SOUP   **Pumpkin** LATKES   **Pumpkin** KUGEL   GENERAL
TSO'S CHICKEN (SPICY)

Your Own Additions

_____

_____

_____

_____

_____

while peeling pumpkins in bed
you can watch Regis + Kathie Lee

It's Halloween
While still in bed, peel pumpkins for pumpkin stew.

Wake up late today. 4:30 A.M.—Practice being scared and tone down scaring others.

Watch out today and prepare yourself for children dressing like you in the Halloween parade.

5:00 A.M.—Drink tea from pumpkin skin with 2 teaspoons of instant coffee.

5:15 A.M.—Start making trick-or-treat bags out of freeze-dried pumpkins from year before.

6:00 A.M.—Get into your costume of a sugar-glazed fruit wreath. Yes, you can still work in it! Remember to wet face and hair and sugar-coat too.

6:30 A.M.—Go to cellar for apples for apple bob. No one will do it, but it sure makes a nice presentation for the foyer.

6:45 A.M.—Start making those damn pumpkin pies.

you can still WASH DISHES IN YOUR SUGAR GLAZED WREATH COSTUME just wrap yourself IN A HEFTY TRASH BAG, Remember open up a space for **your head/face!**

7:45 A.M.—Start making your own witches' brooms from dried brush you collected from Salem, Massachusetts.

8:15 A.M.—Breakfast for 50. Bake marshmallow ghost pancakes that are life-size. Guests wear the ghost pancake and eat themselves out of it.

10:00 A.M.—Antique stores are open. Buy antique washing basin for apple bob.

10:45 A.M.—Can't find antique washtub. Buy new one and antique.

11:20 A.M.—I HATE DAYS LIKE THESE. I'M NOT DOING ENOUGH!

11:30 A.M.—Squeeze in another pie.

12:15 P.M.—Start cleaning out refrigerator for haunted house. Keep bad smells in fridge. Keep moldy apple sauce, sour milk, old, forgotten—gee, I can't even recognize it anymore, but I think it used to be meat. Throw out all good food. Take off door and let kids and grown-ups go in for haunted house. Throw a few spiderwebs in. Turn off lights. My fridge can hold six 200-pound adults comfortably.

12:45 P.M.—Lunch. I guess I can eat at McDonald's this once.

1:45 P.M.—In butter cream frosting write the name of every student from the local school on the 500 pumpkin cupcakes I made today but forgot to write down. I've got to get more organized! Deliver in costume of giant rat made from real rat hides found in the subways of New York City.

2:30 P.M.—Start tying up little ghosts made out of pH-neutral acid-free parchment. Tie up in trees by the time the children get out of school. I've got plenty of time. Do some catalogue shopping for craft supplies for Christmas while I'm at it

3:30 P.M.—Deliver pumpkin fudge to neighborhood.

4:00 P.M.—Carve 150 pumpkins to line winding driveway. Each pumpkin should be carved from plans drawn in July. Set up mannequins made from pumpkins.

5:00 P.M.—Make an intimate dinner for 24. I didn't invite anyone, but it's good practice and I love the menu.

6:00 P.M.—Trick-or-treaters—pass out the homemade candy skeletons made from equal parts of cornstarch, peppermint essence, and yogurt.

7:00 P.M.—Walk around the house with a glass of homemade pumpkin wine and try out bobbing for apples.

7:30 P.M.—100 guests arrive in costume for the Halloween party. I'm dressed as a vase of hydrangeas. Serve recipes from my book *Don't Get Scared in the Kitchen—Halloween the Long Way*. Serve pumpkin-spiced rum punch in hand-blown mugs I made from my book *Stop Breaking Glass, Start Making Glass*. Serve Swedish pumpkin meatballs, but first guests have to pick their own pumpkin in my pumpkin patch and clean out to serve the food in. While guests are in pumpkin patch, put finishing touches on Thanksgiving hand-embroidered table-cloth. It's always the next project. Nothing is ever finished, and there is so much to start!

11:00 P.M.—Before going to sleep, use pumpkin cold creme to clean your face. Recipe from my book *Don't Throw Anything Away! There're Cosmetics in That Garbage!*

my
costume—
I
greeted
my
guests
as
a
vase
of
hydrangeas

Leaf Blowers

There are many things that upset me, whether it's the irritating way that someone slurps a cup of coffee or the denial of a request for bulkhead seating when I travel with my baby, or receiving a computerized phone call. But ever since I've been living out here in the suburbs, I've been waiting for the chance to tell America that especially in October, I hate, despise, just plain can't stand leaf blowers, and I want to try to convince leaf-blower owners to change their ways. What I need to do is to present using a leaf blower as just not good for you, like staying out in the sun too long or being seen with asbestos or as an embarrassment, like spitting and belching in the face of someone who is trying to hire you.

I want to tell you folks that you look really stupid waving and walking with that overgrown hair dryer on your lawn. Everyone who passes you is laughing, for you're blowing those damn grass clippings and you are not getting anywhere. I know that I'm risking not being invited to a few barbecues this summer, but I have to say that I would put leaf blowers in the same category that I have car alarms—noisy things that don't solve the problem that they're supposed to. Leaf blowers make such a racket and all they do is blow air out and spread the leaves and litter into a new area until the wind comes and they're back where they started.

The most successful use of the leaf blower seems to be blowing all the leaves into a pile in the street and then letting the wind carry them to a neighbor's yard. Some of my neighbors own leaf blowers and they just blow the leaves back and forth onto each other's property. Have you ever noticed how banks and other businesses with parking lots hire professional leaf blowers to come at midnight and blow the leaves and debris onto other businesses? And they come with their backwards vacuums and they're supposed to be sneaky about it, but it wakes up the entire neighborhood.

Have you ever tried talking to someone who's using a leaf blower?

You can't. They have headphones on to protect their ears while the rest of us just have to live through the high-pitched velocity of sheer madness.

Sometimes I just want to yell at them, "WHAT THE HELL IS WRONG WITH A RAKE?" Get those wrists going by not using an electric can opener or self-winding watch. Get those arms and legs going by not using the remote control one day a week. No wonder this country has a weight problem.

I'm not saying that you have to use a rake, but rather that you save the leaves. There's a project in those leaves. Save the leaves to make a giant wreath around your roof with ribbon that changes color with the season or make your own dried-leaf dog beds. More leaves? Make more dog beds and more wreaths. Leaves make great toilet paper. Instead of having a roll, just put a leaf bag by the toilet. They'll get the idea. Watch out for poison oak.

I'M GOING TO GET THAT BEASTLY ELM LEAF IF IT TAKES ME ALL DAY

NOVEMBER

DINNER IS SERVED!

And that means...

1. First, we'll have a few beers
2. We'll eat it in our laps - forget plates
3. CAN'T WE WAIT TIL HALF TIME?
4. I'M STUFFED WITH ONION DIP AND DORITO.
5. I LIKE MY TURKEY COLD
6. FOOD ALWAYS TASTES BETTER THE NEXT D₁
7. We'll eat during a commercial
8. WE'll eat when it's over
9. CATCH IT!
10. RUN FOR IT! Oh, NO! TACKLE!

Every year I get letters from my readers complaining about a misery that I will also share with you. The misery that we spend months planning our holiday meals and hours preparing the food, yet it takes only a few minutes to gulp it down and then our guests return to the football game. I know that we experience a great postpartum depression when we see our guests chow down on food that took us so much time and love to prepare.

Picking up the cleaned plates and staring at the guests who have returned to the TV room can usually put the idea in my mind— "I'll impress them next year." But next year comes around and still the moment that we look forward to and long for—the questioning about the selection of our spices, our cooking methods, the oh-so-perfect timing of the entire meal, the table setting in its splendor and finery—and the food is merely gulped down. When the first bite is taken we hope for the beautiful sound of the oohs and ahhs as they taste the food, but it never happens.

I refuse to be hospitalized another year for depression. It's a bad time right after Thanksgiving because Christmas is next and there is so much to do! So I've come up with this solution for the Thanksgiving menu that gives us all the satisfactions of creating but allows our guests to drink the menu down!

Turkey Brew

I've found my Turkey Brew to satisfy the craziness of Thanksgiving. I make all of my goodies in August. Then freeze. Defrost the day before Thanksgiving and throw everything into the blender together.

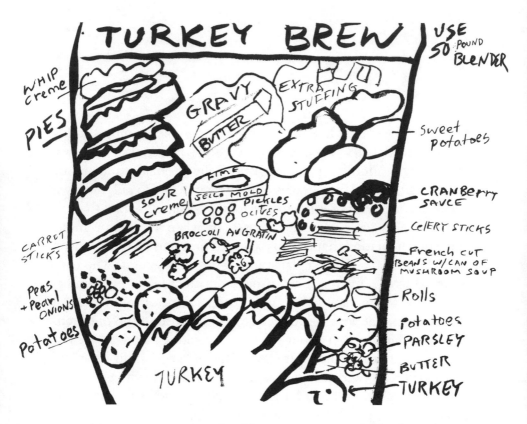

To start: Everyone should own a 50-pound blender. They are hard to find, but I am going to have them included in my Kitchen-Blender-of-the-Month Club soon. I start with a 20-pound tom turkey cooked and stuffed from my book Thanksgiving, Our Yearly Pilgrimage *(in an encyclopedic edition!). Put the turkey in the bottom of the blender, giblets, bones, skin, and all. Add 5 pounds of potatoes. No need to mash those babies. Aren't blenders great? I told you you'd love this.*

Next add butter, parsley, and sour cream. Then 5 pounds of baked sweet potatoes with plenty of butter. I like to put my rolls in next. Don't use store-bought rolls, the dough gets too pasty and the blender doesn't mix well. Follow this with the vegetables—peas with pearl onions, broccoli au gratin, and French-cut frozen beans with a can of mushroom soup.

You thought I forgot the appetizer? Well, I didn't. In goes the carrot and celery sticks, olives without the pits, bread and butter pickles (watch out for the pickle juice or else the whole thing can sour).

What's Thanksgiving without turkey and what's turkey without cranberry sauce? Pretty lousy. Be sure to make fresh cranberry sauce with orange slices and whole sticks of cinnamon. Cut sugar in half when you are making Turkey Brew. A lime Jell-O mold with a little tinned fruit cocktail tastes great in this Turkey Brew!

I know what you've been waiting for—the pies. Put them in—spiced apple, mincemeat, pecan. Sorry, but I can't look at another pumpkin pie because of last month, so I'm not putting one in. But you can if you just can't get enough pumpkin (or if you still have any pumpkin left over). DON'T ADD CHOCO-LATE ANYTHING! It's too overwhelming. But you can add a tiny bit of whipped cream; 5 tablespoons per person.

To complete your Turkey Brew, blend all the above ingredients on high for 2 minutes. Stop to scrape sides with rubber spatula. Add 1 quart of vodka. Mix again on high for 30 seconds. Serve over ice in highball glasses. Garnish with fresh sprigs of sage or sprinkles of dried sage. If you prefer, the brew can be warmed up in a microwave for those guests who have to have something warm in their stomachs.

Are you sick of dirty dishes? Well, there is NO MESS here except a 50-pound blender to clean. I just take mine out to the backyard and hose it down. Guests can sit around the table gulping, slurping down their drinks. And there are no dishes to wash. Now, that's a holiday!

Games People Play

Trying to entertain the little nieces and nephews on Thanksgiving doesn't have to be difficult. After they have helped me polish, vacuum, and dust, I bring out a game called plastic surgery. I have a big picture of Michael Jackson's face (as it originally looked as a teenager) pasted to a piece of cardboard and I have cutouts of other people's eyes, ears, noses, cheekbones, lips, etc. The kids then take turns trying to see who can make his face look like it does today. Big fun!

Michael is so weird, but we still can't get enough of him. If he's good enough for Liz and Lisa Marie, he's good enough for us. He's like Peter Pan with an angry inner child. Using his name is helpful, though, when my little ones are drinking too much Pepsi—I tell them that their head will explode into flames like Michael Jackson's did, and then I show them the videotape of his hair getting torched while he's got a Pepsi in his hand. That keeps them out of the kitchen for a few days.

Political Plastering

November also means election time. So what better time to make an addition to my presidential hallway. My grand entrance hallway is plastered with trowel strokes inspired by presidents. For example, a swooping ski-jump-nose stroke for Nixon, peanut-shaped strokes for Jimmy Carter, and interpreting the rounded bottom of Rubenesque Bill Clinton. I'd like to share with you how I came to the creation of my presidential hallway.

I began by covering the floor with the last few issues of the Sunday *New York Times*. I have the paper delivered and I actu-

Rainy Day Activities
on Michael Jackson

1. DAYDREAM —

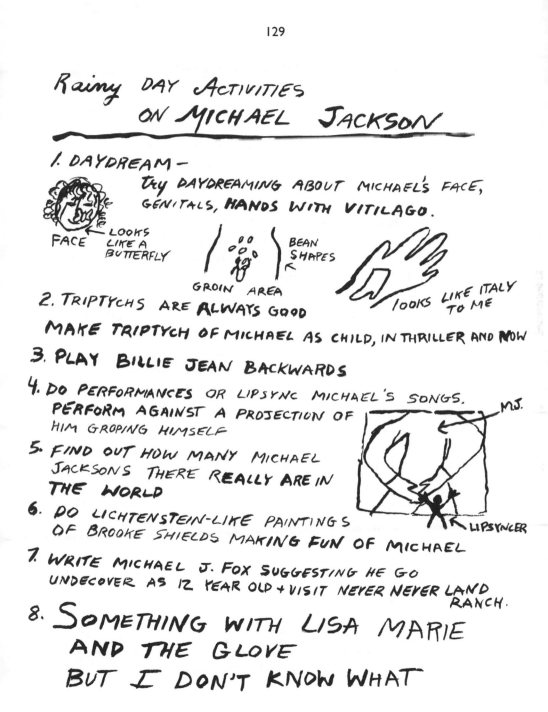

Try DAYDREAMING ABOUT MICHAEL'S FACE, GENITALS, **HANDS WITH VITILAGO.**

FACE ← LOOKS LIKE A BUTTERFLY

GROIN AREA

BEAN SHAPES

looks LIKE ITALY TO ME

2. TRIPTYCHS ARE ALWAYS GOOD

MAKE TRIPTYCH OF MICHAEL AS CHILD, IN THRILLER AND NOW

3. PLAY BILLIE JEAN BACKWARDS

4. DO PERFORMANCES OR LIPSYNC MICHAEL'S SONGS. PERFORM AGAINST A PROJECTION OF HIM GROPING HIMSELF

5. FIND OUT HOW MANY MICHAEL JACKSONS THERE **REALLY ARE IN THE WORLD**

M.J.

LIPSYNCER

6. DO LICHTENSTEIN-LIKE PAINTINGS OF BROOKE SHIELDS MAKING FUN OF MICHAEL

7. WRITE MICHAEL J. FOX SUGGESTING HE GO UNDECOVER AS 12 YEAR OLD + VISIT NEVER NEVER LAND RANCH.

8. SOMETHING WITH LISA MARIE AND THE GLOVE BUT I DON'T KNOW WHAT

ally never seem to have time to read it, but it looks great sitting out in front of my house all morning every Sunday. Anyway, with its large pages, it makes the best floor covering for my craft projects.

I started to plaster, but I just couldn't seem to get the strokes the way I wanted them with my trowel. I realized that I lacked inspiration. I hung my head in dejection and was staring down at the paper-covered floor, when it hit me! There was President Clinton on the front page of the *Times* in his jogging shorts! That quivering derriere! He would be my inspiration much like the classical painters had their models. What a lovely result. My textured walls look fabulous and I have Bill Clinton's tush to thank for it.

The following week we had the neighbors over for a party to show off the new plastering. Everyone loved my booty-shaped trowel strokes. And it was funny how the conversation turned to politics without ever mentioning my source for inspiration.

You can write words in the plaster to describe the president. I chose "adult child of an alcoholic," "people pleaser," and the sentence "It's O.K. to tell the world that you are embarrassed by your brother."

My friend Barbara, who does makeovers at Bloomie's, said that what the first couple really needs is a makeover. That gave me the idea to paint the walls as an Italian fresco with Bill and Hillary as my subject. She thinks that since they are baby boomers they should definitely do sixties. I have painted Hillary in a lime-green paisley granny dress with daisy beads made by Chelsea. Now, you know they must have been tripping when they named her Chelsea. Yes, Hillary is braless and barefoot in my fresco.

I solve Hillary and Bill's hair problems by painting their hair long, wild, and messy. It couldn't be any worse than those other coifs sported. I then paint Bill with a hippie look. I paint a tie-dyed Grateful Dead T-shirt that reads PIG PEN LIVES on Bill with him

Plastering Patterns
Based on Bill Clinton's Derriere

Makeover for Bill

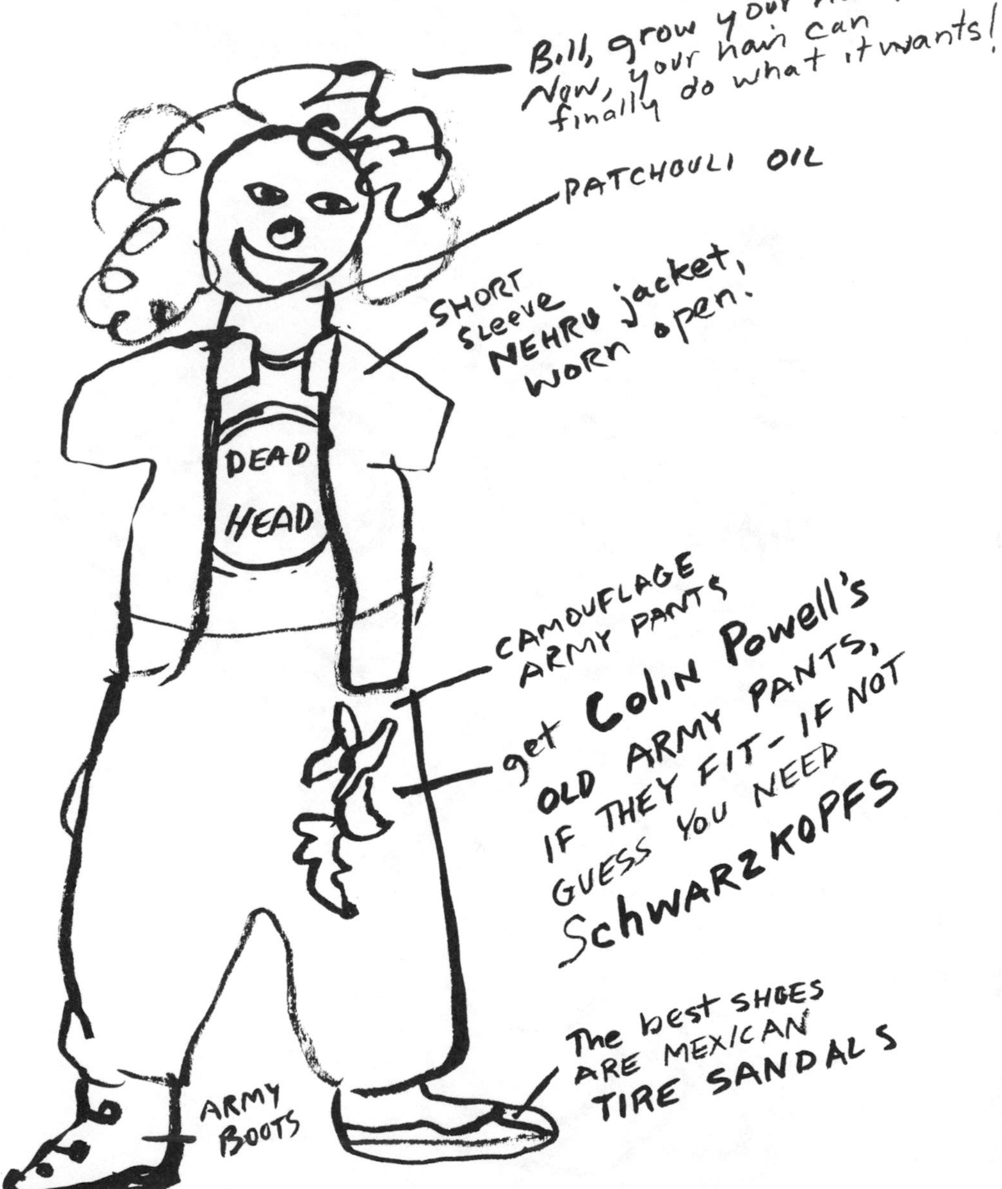

Bill, grow your hair!
Now, your hair can
finally do what it wants!

PATCHOULI OIL

SHORT
SLEEVE
NEHRU jacket,
worn open.

DEAD HEAD

CAMOUFLAGE
ARMY PANTS

get Colin Powell's
OLD ARMY PANTS,
IF THEY FIT- IF NOT
GUESS YOU NEED
SCHWARZKOPFS

The best shoes
ARE MEXICAN
TIRE SANDALS

ARMY
BOOTS

Make Over for Hillary

IRON HAIR

OR — Let HAIR GO — PART IN MIDDLE — HENNA ORANGE lots of braids

granny glasses

NO BRA, let it hang girl

HAVE CHELSEA MAKE YOU DAISY NECKLACES

BELL SLEEVES

KNAPSACK

go barefoot in Whitehouse

wearing a pair of Colin Powell's army fatigues. OOPS! They don't fit, better paint on Schwarzkopf's. Bill would look great wearing Mexican tire sandals. I paint a Nehru jacket on Bill, and he's ready for Camp David.

You can use this concept for past and future presidents.

December

The most memorable Christmases are the ones that are ruined. It's a real art to be able to invite just the right amount of sibling rivalry and drunkenness with overall holiday hesitation and guilt to provide a good time for all. The idea is to invite unresolved conflict and resolve it right at your dinner table. That will make the food more memorable.

Start by inviting friends or family that you have had an argument with recently and tell them you intend to bury the hatchet at this year's holidays. Ask if they would please join you for dinner. When they accept, the stage is set for a memorable holiday for years to come. Also invite family members who have been squabbling and are seeing one another in your living room for the very first time since the argument. Now, that is no easy accomplishment, I might add, and I do add.

One method that I use when inviting guests is to think of the Hundred-Acre Wood and its residents for a good overall psychological profile. Think of yourself as Christopher Robin, the enabler. Invite someone like Winnie-the-Pooh with an eating disorder. Invite a passive-aggressive type like Rabbit. Get that mother-attachment thing happening like with a Kanga and a Roo. Add an insecure guest with low self-esteem like Piglet, mix in a know-it-all such as Owl, and a manic-depressive such as Tigger. Now, that's what I call a guest list.

Here are some pointers to ensure a memorable holiday:

KEEP THE HOLIDAY MEMORABLE
GET THE GUEST IN THE KITCHEN

1. Once the guests have arrived. Everyone needs some warming up and here is the guaranteed ice breaker I use and it works every time: kindly ask your squabbling guests to reenact their disagreement.

2. Always have plenty of alcoholic beverages on hand.

3. Continue repetitive prodding questions about the original argument.

4. If you have to, take a side.

5. If still nothing is happening, quietly take a guest to the kitchen and tell her you can side with her position.

6. While they are brewing and stewing, now is the time to start making fun of siblings like you did as children.

7. Start calling sibling names that were used as children (i.e., Jowls, Stutter Butter).

8. Make that scapegoat work his holiday! Go to past incidents where the sibling made a fool of himself.

9. Always invite non-family members. A good heated moment is when a family member tells a non-family member, "Do you want to hear about the time my brother put my Barbie doll in the toilet and it wasn't number 1 in there? When the non-family member says "not really," we know that is when we are on the way to a truly unforgettable holiday experience.

10. At this point yell out "Dinner!" so that no one can leave. The big fear of Christmas is to be alone and forgotten and have no food, so no matter what happens, your guests won't leave. Always have your guests wait for food. Not eating always makes the crankiness edge go up.

11. Still, if no guests have had an outburst, start telling embarrassing stories about your guests. This time talk about the non-family members and try to get your family to gang up on your guests. Go around the table till dessert and coffee. Hopefully, by this time someone passes out, pukes, or breaks something.

DON'T WORRY, THEY WILL ALL BE BACK NEXT YEAR!

Your Christmas Holiday Monthly Checklist. The Rush Is On. Only 51 Weeks Till Christmas.

January——Start making handmade carved icicles from glued sugar cubes. Make 15,000. The icicles will hang from every ceiling in the house. You are the mastermind of an entire empire called Winter Wonderland. The theme is yours. The control is yours. Go with it! Remember, the clock is ticking toward the big competition to show the world what we can do to a holiday.

February——Should have 250 hand-crocheted snowflakes finished. Start weaving snowflake toilet seat cover with matching toothbrush holder. Do two sets for when one gets dirty. Do another bathroom set—bathmat, towels, toilet seat cover. Do the toothbrush holder in the theme of holly for your guest bathroom. It feels

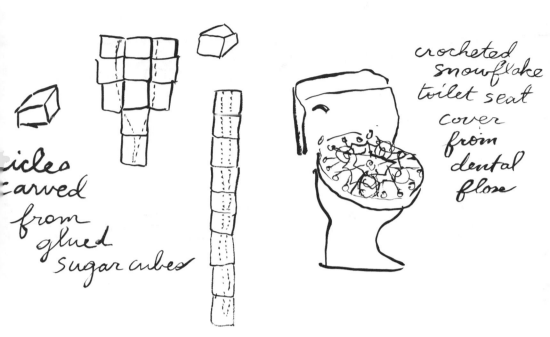

icles carved from glued sugar cubes

crocheted snowflake toilet seat cover from dental floss

good when the bathrooms are finished for the holidays. Make hooked rug for the living room to the theme of the twelve days of Christmas.

March—is the month to finish your snow-scene village. Make traffic signals and street lamps from the old toothbrushes you have collected from around the neighborhood. Make sure there is some graffiti art in your snow village! Empty juice boxes glued together makes some great condominiums! Remember the security gates. People look for detail. There is always going to be some wiseguy cracking, "Where are the doorbells on your houses in the snow village?" Hear what I'm saying? Start wiring for sound. This is the month to do it. Better to do it now than while guests are arriving on Christmas Eve.

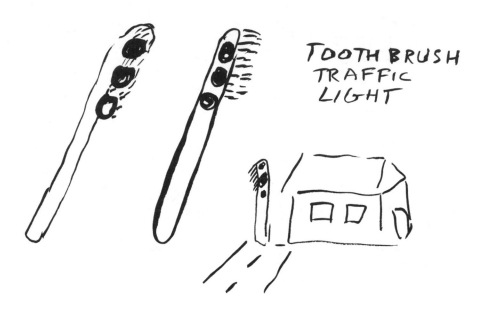

April—Hand-paint a new set of holiday china. This year I'm painting all the countries from around the world and how they decorate their trees. And you thought I wasn't into education.

Tie up house like a Christmas-wrapped gift. If you don't have the room, make the room!

May—Don't think you can get out of it. You need to make brand-new Christmas stockings every year. This includes making stockings for your grocer, your postman, and your dentist besides your family and pets. The secret to a good holiday handicraft year is to make things for people you barely know.

This year I'm taking my ordinary dried macaroni and individually covering them in forest-green velvet. What am I doing with these velvet-covered macaronis? Hell if I know, but they just might come in handy!

macaroni in green velvet

June—Time to go and select your Christmas tree. You have got to get out there before Rockefeller Center does. They are getting all the best trees, and that just can't happen. Go to the forest, cut your own forty-foot tree, and put it in the freezer. I always have an extra tree in the freezer. Just in case. My life is about "just in case." And I got a handle on it.

Don't keep that door open too long—There's trees in this freezer!

40 FT

July——Start testing the outdoor lights on a weekly basis starting now, so you can monitor how much flak you will get from the neighbors.

Remove last year's dried poinsettias from books. You will use them to make your own handmade Christmas cards. Yes, it takes a lot of poinsettias, but you have them growing in your greenhouse if you run out. And then just microwave on high until crisply done. Remember?

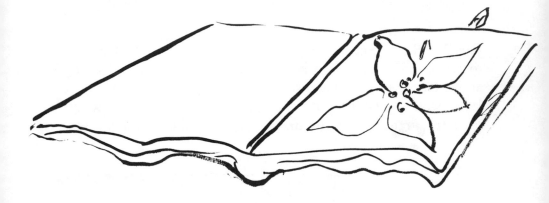

August——Never get a chance to make all the holiday cookies you want? Start making a batch a day and freeze.

Make holiday soaps from scratch. Pine, eggnog, and hollyberry are all good.

in August start making a batch of cookies a day!

September—START DECORATING THE HOUSE NOW!

October—This is a big month. You should have all your outdoor lights up by the fifteenth. Don't let the stores start decorating before you do! All your first-floor windows should be dioramas with moving holiday scenes. This year do *The Nutcracker* in the windows with movable dolls. The music from *The Nutcracker* can be loudspeakered outside. Outdoor figurines include Rudolph and reindeer and Santa in sleigh on roof, Mr. and Mrs. Snowman and their little snowmen. (Gee, that Snowman name is a bit sexist.) Have MERRY CHRISTMAS written in lights on roof as well. Have marching soldiers in front yard, at least forty. From trees hang twelve-foot-high angels. I do six twelve-foot lit angels in pale yellow, iridescent pink and blue, white, a deep blue, and a magenta. The magenta angel should be placed more in the center. Yes, I have a manger scene with real animals and actors. You can get actors for cheap. They want the work. Animals aren't so easy. Make animal costumes out of sheets. You have time. That is why we start in April for problems like these. It feels so good when a problem comes up and we can take care of it. We are ready for it. I also have on my front lawn a giant Christmas stocking that should be the size of your house. I'm taking it easy this year on the outside, so this is all I'm doing on my outdoor lights and figures.

November—Go to doctor for Valium. The extra rush is here. Sometimes I almost can't take it. But I always do. Oh my god, I can feel the pressure, the adrenaline, the crisis, the energy, the big meal, people I love to hate, people I hate to love. It's almost the time.

November is emotion month. Are you emotional enough for this holiday? Get some edge to you. Or it could happen! No one will remember the way you celebrate—and at all costs that cannot happen!

Start practicing
wearing the
SANTA SUIT AND
cleaning the
house - for
believability.
you can't
fool
kids
these days!

December—Caroling, shopping, wrapping, buying, baking, buffeting, partying, cooking, the children's party, the tree-trimming party, the party at work, Christmas cards, sewing and wearing the Santa suit, ornaments, get the mistletoe up, make wreaths out of flowers, herbs, oranges, and pomegranates, pine cones and calico, the gingerbread house, the Christmas sweater with three trees and stars, Santa Claus everywhere, put tassels, make strands of popcorn and cranberries and, hey, strand that velvet-covered macaroni, stencil angels on the walls, have bells everywhere, get the music on, cookies out, fruitcake made, cheese logs ready, gifts wrapped, menus prepared, centerpiece designed, apron embroidered with the song "I Wish You a Merry Christmas," please invite someone named Noel to your house, write to Santa, start using words like "Jack Frost" and "jolly," put some pine cones in glitter and casually lay around the house, the fireplace mantel must be a place of glory, star candles, make Santa napkin rings, doorknob covers with Rudolph's red nose, paint an angel on that dustpan— I DEMAND CHRISTMAS EVERYWHERE!, make a Christmas tree out of birdseed for the birds, dried hydrangea Christmas trees everywhere—please spray gold and silver—THESE IDEAS ARE GETTING ME EXCITED. Christmas means pillows with candy canes, make our own candy canes from my book Yes, YOU CAN MAKE CANDY LIKE I CAN. It's time to make gifts—personalized haiku on needlepoint pillows, and. . . . REMEMBER, THIS WHOLE MONTH IS LAST-MINUTE!

Acknowledgments

I would like to thank Dino Moraitis, who died of AIDS in 1993, for his initial suggestion to do this book; Ann Patty, Peter Ginsberg, Bruce Tracy, David Cole, David Lerner, and Mary D. Dorman.

I would like to acknowledge the following for their inspiration: Muney Rivers, for her plastic flower garden; Colleen Colbert and Joel Carreiro for discussions and insight on Winnie the Pooh; Jay Critchley, artist, who makes incredible art out of plastic tampon applicators; David Wojnarowicz, artist, who died of AIDS in 1992, for his creation of cockabunnies: gluing paper bunny ears and tails on cockroaches; and Astrith and Felicia Deyrup, for their knowledge of nature and life.

About the Author

Karen Finley was born in Chicago, received a Master of Fine Arts degree from the San Francisco Art Institute, and currently lives outside of New York City. She is a visual and performance artist and also writes and directs plays, appears in films, and has authored two books, *Shock Treatment* and *Enough Is Enough.* She has had numerous installations and presentations of her performances throughout North and South America, Europe, and Australia.

sweeping buffing dusting polishing waxing
vacuuming baking beating blending chopping grating slicing dicing mixing
making cleaning cooking freezing
squeezing peeling blanching boi-
ling broiling roasting broasting
simmering steaming sauteeing
poaching frying browning burning oiling creaming folding
whipping pureeing icing frosting adding cooling measuring
scooping scrubbing stacking sorting
starching scalding bleaching
folding ironing straightening
washing hemming mending
crocheting knitting quilting knot-
ting macrame embroidering
sewing needlepointing stitching
soaking drying hanging all done